A WORLD IN NEED OF LEADERSHIP: TOMORROW'S UNITED NATIONS

– A Fresh Appraisal –

Brian Urquhart
and
Erskine Childers

DAG HAMMARSKJÖLD FOUNDATION
UPPSALA, SWEDEN
1996

▶ Contents

CHAPTER THREE: CONCLUSIONS AND RECOMMENDATIONS

▶ **Diagrams and Tables**

Brian
Urquhart

Erskine
Childers

A WORLD IN NEED
OF LEADERSHIP:
TOMORROW'S UNITED NATIONS
– A FRESH APPRAISAL –

THE UNITED NATIONS SYSTEM

PRINCIPAL ORGANS OF THE UNITED NATIONS

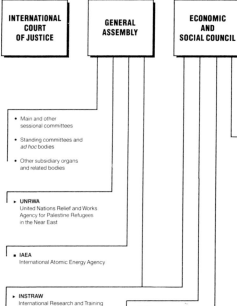

INTERNATIONAL COURT OF JUSTICE	GENERAL ASSEMBLY	ECONOMIC AND SOCIAL COUNCIL	SECURITY COUNCIL	SECRETARIAT	TRUSTEESHIP COUNCIL

- Military Staff Committee
- Standing committees and *ad hoc* bodies

- Main and other sessional committees
- Standing committees and *ad hoc* bodies
- Other subsidiary organs and related bodies

► UNRWA
United Nations Relief and Works Agency for Palestine Refugees in the Near East

■ IAEA
International Atomic Energy Agency

► INSTRAW
International Research and Training Institute for the Advancement of Women

► UNCHS
United Nations Centre for Human Settlements (Habitat)

► UNCTAD
United Nations Conference on Trade and Development

► UNDP
United Nations Development Programme

► UNEP
United Nations Environment Programme

► UNFPA
United Nations Population Fund

► UNHCR
Office of the United Nations High Commissioner for Refugees

► UNICEF
United Nations Children's Fund

► UNIFEM
United Nations Development Fund for Women

► UNITAR
United Nations Institute for Training and Research

► UNU
United Nations University

► WFC
World Food Council

► UNDCP
United Nations International Drug Control Programme

► WFP
World Food Programme

► ITC
International Trade Centre UNCTAD/GATT

• FUNCTIONAL COMMISSIONS
Commission for Social Development
Commission on Human Rights
Commission on Narcotic Drugs
Commission on the Status of Women
Population Commission
Statistical Commission

• REGIONAL COMMISSIONS
Economic Commission for Africa (ECA)
Economic Commission for Europe (ECE)
Economic Commission for Latin America and the Caribbean (ECLAC)
Economic and Social Commission for Asia and the Pacific (ESCAP)
Economic and Social Commission for Western Asia (ESCWA)

• SESSIONAL AND STANDING COMMITTEES

• EXPERT, *AD HOC* AND RELATED BODIES

■ ILO
International Labour Organisation

■ FAO
Food and Agriculture Organisation of the United Nations

■ UNESCO
United Nations Educational, Scientific and Cultural Organisation

■ WHO
World Health Organisation

World Bank Group

■ IBRD
International Bank for Reconstruction and Development (World Bank)

■ IDA
International Development Association

■ IFC
International Finance Corporation

■ IMF
International Monetary Fund

■ ICAO
International Civil Aviation Organisation

■ UPU
Universal Postal Union

■ ITU
International Telecommunication Union

■ WMO
World Meteorological Organisation

■ IMO
International Maritime Organisation

■ WIPO
World Intellectual Property Organisation

■ IFAD
International Fund for Agricultural Development

■ UNIDO
United Nations Industrial Development Organisation

■ (GATT/WTO
The General Agreement on Tariffs and Trade, which had informal Agency status, has been replaced by the World Trade Organization; no UN status has been agreed for WTO to date)

Peace-keeping operations*

► UNTSO
United Nations Truce Supervision Organisation
June 1948 to present

► UMMOGIP
United Nations Military Observer Group in India and Pakistan
January 1949 to present

► UNFICYP
United Nations Peace-keeping Force in Cyprus
March 1964 to present

► UNDOF
United Nations Disengagement Observer Force
June 1974 to present

► UNIFIL
United Nations Interim Force in Lebanon
March 1978 to present

► UNIKOM
United Nations Iraq-Kuwait Observation Mission
April 1991 to present

► UNAVEM II
United Nations Angola Verification Mission II
June 1991 to present

► ONUSAL
United Nations Observer Mission in El Salvador
July 1991 to present

► MINURSO
United Nations Mission for the Referendum in Western Sahara
September 1991 to present

► UNPROFOR
United Nations Protection Force
March 1992 to present

► UNTAC
United Nations Transnational Authority in Cambodia
March 1992 to present

► UNOSOM
United Nations Operation in Somalia
April 1992 to present

► ONUMOZ
United Nations Operation in Mozambique
December 1992 to present

► UNOMUR
United Nation Observer Mission Uganda-Rwanda
June 1993 to present

► UNOMIL
United Nation Observer Mission in Liberia
August 1993 to present

► United Nations programmes and organs (representative list only)
■ Specialized agencies and other autonomous organizations within the system
• Other commissions, committees and *ad hoc* and related bodies

*Subject to frequent change; citations are indicative only

PREFACE

As the 1990s opened, it was clear that the dramatic changes taking place in the world would require imaginative and courageous leadership from the United Nations. Yet the selection of the leaders of the principal international organizations, including the Secretary-General of the United Nations by member governments, continued to be haphazard, far less searching or systematic than any small university's procedures for choosing a new president. In 1990 we offered an analysis of these leadership problems in the UN and its agencies, which was published by the Dag Hammarskjöld Foundation (in *Development Dialogue* 1990:1-2) under joint sponsorship with the Ford Foundation.

That study resulted in discussions among Permanent Representatives to the UN at the time, and even some informal discussions in the Security Council. However, no changes in the selection process, nor changes in such closely related factors as length of term, were agreed upon.

Six years later the UN and the agencies of the system face ever grimmer and more complex challenges as the tumultuous nature of the post-Cold War world has revealed itself. Demands upon UN leadership have greatly increased, especially in respect of peace, human security and human rights, while it is more important than ever to tackle the socio-economic causes of upheavals and instability which now afflict the world.

In re-issuing this study we hope to draw renewed attention to a problem that will not go away through neglect. We have found no reason to change either our basic analysis or our recommendations, but this second edition has been revised to take account of new factors and to suggest some further actions for governments to consider. In addition, to deepen the analysis of the leadership question in the Specialized Agencies, the Ford Foundation made possible a study of the elections of Directors-General of the Food and Agriculture Organization of the United Nations (FAO), by Charles Weitz, a veteran of the UN system. We have greatly benefited from his analysis and observations which are excerpted and cited herein. His full study will also be published in 1996 by the Dag Hammarskjöld Foundation as a companion work.

This second edition begins with a summary analysis with recommendations concerning the post of Secretary-General. It is followed by a chapter amplifying the arguments and reasoning underlying the main paper, looking more at leadership in the UN system as a whole, and examining the arrangements needed for optimum leadership. The original compilation of statistical data on UN leadership posts has been brought up to date, in tables placed in the relevant chapters. All recommendations are assembled in a final chapter.

We express our appreciation to the Ford Foundation for its support over the years, and in particular to Shepard Forman, the director of the international program at the Foundation. We have acknowledged in the 1990 edition those who gave research and other support. We thank Marjolijn Snippe for all statistical and other professional research for this edition.

Brian
Urquhart

Erskine
Childers

*A   WORLD   IN   NEED
OF   LEADERSHIP :
TOMORROW'S   UNITED   NATIONS
- A   FRESH   APPRAISAL -*

We must also once again acknowledge with gratitude the enduring contribution of the original steering group for the first edition, whose names were listed in it along with the large international panel of experts for whose comments on that edition we also remain most grateful. However, we wish to make it clear that responsibility for the opinions and recommendations in this edition, as in the first, is solely that of the authors.

Finally, we wish to reiterate our gratitude to Olle Nordberg and Sven Hamrell of the Dag Hammarskjöld Foundation, and their staff colleagues, who have so creatively, expeditiously and stylishly published all our studies. They have also given generously of their wise counsel throughout the process.

This study is re-issued in a year when governments are seriously considering measures to strengthen the United Nations, and when they must once again face up to their responsibilities for its leadership. We hope that the study may be helpful to them and also prove of benefit to the peoples of the United Nations whom they serve.

New York and Geneva, June 1996   *Brian Urquhart*   *Erskine Childers*

CHAPTER ONE

UNITED NATIONS LEADERSHIP

I. *INTRODUCTION*

A World in Need of Leadership: Tomorrow's United Nations was first published nearly six years ago at a time of great optimism about the United Nations. We stated then that a successful response to the new challenges being presented to the United Nations system of organizations 'will depend in considerable measure on the capacity and quality of their leadership'. We pointed out that such leadership would be needed 'to bring divergent interests together, and to generate ideas large and practical enough to match and manage new global developments'. It would also be needed for the reform and even the restructuring of the existing international system.

Six years later the climate for international cooperation has badly deteriorated. The post-Cold War world has proved complex and violent, and some of the UN's new commitments have proved to be quagmires or even failures. A striking absence of leadership both at the national and the international level has generated skepticism about international organizations in many quarters. Domestic financial constraints and current ideological aversion to governmental institutions have both been instrumental in reducing support for the UN system.

The costs of the system for all its economic and social, political and peace work are minuscule by any disinterested measurement (about $2 per year per human being alive on Earth). Nonetheless, many activities which until recently were considered vital to the peoples of the world have undergone crippling reductions. Even more serious are signs in influential quarters of an emerging neo-isolationism and a distaste for multilateral action, trends which echo similar movements in the 1920s and 1930s that had disastrous consequences for the world.

In the past five years there has been an increasing tendency to assign vital and complex tasks to the UN without providing the leadership, the resources or the authority to tackle them effectively, and then conveniently to blame 'the UN' for the subsequent shortcomings. At the time of writing, the UN—whatever that may mean—is blamed for the collapse of the role assigned to it by the Security Council in Bosnia, for the Council's failure to prevent or halt genocide in Rwanda, and for earlier failures in Somalia. This has led (not for the first time) to proclaiming the necessity to seek solutions elsewhere and even to prophesying the end of UN peace-keeping.

These 'UN failures' are also being used for larger ends. Influential politicians in the United States question the basic rationale of the UN as conceived by President Franklin Roosevelt and his successors: the necessity of collective international action both to maintain international peace and security and to build its foundation by promoting economic and social development

Brian
Urquhart

Erskine
Childers

A   WORLD   IN   NEED
OF   LEADERSHIP :
TOMORROW'S   UNITED   NATIONS
– A   FRESH   APPRAISAL –

for all. Adherents of this ideological trend also seek to garner wider support by incessant attacks on UN management and performance. In fact, the effort to force reform by cutting off funds has brought the UN to a breaking point and is making serious reform and reorganization virtually impossible.

Good administration, expert management, and an international civil service of the highest quality are indeed vital to the future of the world organization. The Secretary-General must be able to work effectively for very difficult objectives, and to delegate authority to carefully selected deputies in order to achieve them. However, in a world where many dangerous problems have been seriously neglected, an exclusive concentration on internal management issues can, and will, seriously distract attention and resources from other major responsibilities.

The United Nations does not have sovereign authority, significant power, or resources of its own. It relies to a great degree for its effectiveness on the ideas and principles in the Charter and the decisions and guidelines adopted by the General Assembly. The Secretary-General is the key executive of these principles and guidelines, and their institutional guardian.

> The Secretary-General, more than anyone else, will stand for the United
> Nations as a whole. In the eyes of the world (he) must embody the
> principles and ideals of the Charter to which the Organization seeks to
> give effect.
>
> *Report of the United Nations Preparatory Commission,*
> *UN document PC/20, 23 December 1945, page 87.*

One test of a Secretary-General is the degree to which he or she can make these ideas and principles understandable and acceptable, not just to governments but to the peoples of the world as well. A second main test concerns guardianship. In a highly disorderly world the UN can be easily abused by poor or self-serving decision-making. On such occasions the Secretary-General cannot merely be 'the servant of the Security Council', but must be prepared to speak out when UN principles or guidelines are being ignored, or when there is a failure to match assigned tasks with adequate mandates and resources.

Dag Hammarskjöld, who succeeded more than any other Secretary-General in articulating the aims and principles of the UN to a world public, spoke of his task as 'working on the edge of the development of human society' to promote 'the creative evolution' of human institutions. He saw the UN as a 'venture in progress towards an international community living in peace under the laws of justice'. The great venture is now in desperate need of inspiring, visionary leadership.

Strong and independent leadership by the Secretary-General is sometimes resented. The UN is an intergovernmental organization, and governments have no intention of giving up control of it. But in times of major crisis, when governments have reached the limits of their own resourcefulness, the Secretary-General can play an indispensable role in clarifying, rallying, and proposing new ways forward. Then, a clear and independent voice can make the vital difference—and this, too, is often missing.

From the very outset, governments have been ambivalent about the role of the Secretary-General and the international civil service, especially in relation to the traditional concept of 'great powers'. The Secretary-General is all too often damned if he does take initiative, and damned if he doesn't. Courageous leadership, new ideas and an independent point of view are sometimes criticized as empire-building or even aspirations for world government. The world at large, however, expects leadership on vital matters from the Secretary-General, who must ultimately be the judge of how far to go.

The choice of the holder of an office that encompasses so many essential international functions should be a matter of the highest priority for governments. At present, however, there seems to be little consensus on looking for a leader, or looking at all beyond a limited group of self-proposed candidates or candidates put forward by their own governments. Indeed it is impossible to escape the impression that many governments, including some of the most powerful, do not in fact want a strong, independent leader as Secretary-General. The record is not much better for other top positions in the UN system. And yet the most frequent criticisms of the UN are of uncertain leadership, poor management, and indifferent performance. If these criticisms have any basis, surely the governments most concerned should be the most diligent about the selection of the leadership.

As many as 25 complex emergencies now threaten tens of millions of people worldwide every year and generate enormous challenges, as well as costs, for the whole international community. The convulsions are becoming larger, and with wider repercussions. This new generation of crises will continue until their underlying causes are properly addressed. Apart from other developments this fact alone reveals the current assault on multilateralism and international solidarity and organization as fatally short-sighted.

The United Nations system needs to be renewed and put into condition to respond to these simultaneous challenges—tackling the causes of conflict and dealing with the violent consequences of their past neglect. Only statesmanship and leadership of the highest order can guide the international community through the current period of anger and upheaval and re-build a more peaceable and just world. This is a matter of vital importance for *all* the peoples of this earth.

II. THE INTERNATIONAL AGENDA FOR THE 1990s

Secretary-General Javier Pérez de Cuellar, in 'Perspectives for the 1990s', sketched out a general agenda for the UN as this decade opened.

> It must be the common purpose to forge from ... varied, sometimes contradictory, economic, social and political conditions, a global environment of sustained development, social justice and peace.

The nations of the world are being forced to take account of this 'global environment' as never before. In this process governments are being more frequently confronted with the necessity to find acceptable ways in which to yield elements of their sovereignty through common actions and codes of conduct, in order to deal with issues which cannot be tackled by one nation, or even one group of nations, alone. There is an increasing awareness that the traditional structures of government are inadequate for a world that is suddenly far more complex and fragile than before.

The proliferation of phenomena which transcend national boundaries—technology, communications, the global financial market, disease, crime and drug trafficking, mass movements of peoples, or environmental pollution, to name only a few—continues unabated. It is combining with the excessive use of resources by one fraction of the population on the one hand, and continuing population increase among the poorest three-quarters of humanity on the other, to produce the most precarious conditions our planet has ever known.

The optimism of earlier decades over the marvels of science and technology has suffered a series of rude ecological awakenings. It is now also clear that technology has not always been closing, and in many cases has even been widening, the gap between the affluent North and much of a poverty-stricken and increasingly restless South.

Too hasty optimism in the North about the 'Green Revolution' caused governments to assume that food security and a strong Food and Agriculture Organization of the UN need no longer have high priority. The same kind of optimism, combined with energetic sales promotion, generated a dangerous reliance on chemical fertilizers. Apart from their ecological damage, since 1990 the use of fertilizers has drastically fallen because grains no longer respond to them; but there is now no early substitute for fertilizer-based grains, and cropland available per capita has not expanded. World food reserves are now lower than they were in the food security crisis of 1974. Yet again, the insistence of Northern advisors that developing countries maintain their colonial-era cash crops for export, combined with the dumping of subsidized Northern food, has resulted in deficient national food production: developing countries' needs of cereal imports will increase by 50 per cent over the next fifteen years. In large parts of the South, poverty and inappropriate external development models which have failed to provide for expanding populations are in turn wreaking ecological degradation.

Phenomena which were once thought to be comfortably controlled or enhanced by science, or neatly self-contained within specialized sectors, or manageable within nation states, have thus emerged as systemically dangerous, multi-sectoral, and transnational hazards. The agenda of the international community has thus enormously expanded—in the number of its items, in their scope and in their interrelationship.

International law, only yesterday a seemingly quiet backwater in human affairs, is reaching into hitherto unimagined fields. The nations of the world have acceded to an unprecedented number of agreements in virtually all branches of human activity—from the ocean floor to the planet's climate to outer space—in only the last forty years. There has been a truly astonishing growth of public international law which will accelerate into the coming century. The pressing need for an international system based on law has never been so evident.

Differences between groups of states on how the international agenda should be realized have not been resolved. The 50th Anniversary of the United Nations did, however, provide the opportunity for some efforts to rethink the United Nations system, which has hitherto been structured largely as a projection of the different sectors of national administrations. Ideas for radical reform are still generally unwelcome in intergovernmental circles. Serious and effective reform and innovation will therefore require both sustained and skilful leadership and a great deal of hard work and constituency building.

Main areas of responsibility for the UN system and its future leadership:

- ▸ the maintenance of early warning systems on potential conflicts, and the conduct of preventive diplomacy;
- ▸ the peaceful settlement of disputes; peace-making (in the UN sense of the term) and peace-keeping;
- ▸ disarmament, arms regulation and reduction of the flow of arms;
- ▸ the promotion of an effective system of common and collective security;
- ▸ the promotion of a more equitable and purposeful management of the world economy;
- ▸ proposals for dealing with the world's financial and monetary problems including the debt problem;
- ▸ the mobilization of resources and the formulation of strategies to overcome mass poverty and marginalization;
- ▸ leadership in safeguarding the environment and in the management of the global commons;
- ▸ the management and mitigation of urgent and major problems, including those posed by refugees and large scale migrations, natural disasters and other human emergencies, AIDS and other diseases, and the international drug problem;

Brian
Urquhart

Erskine
Childers

A   WORLD   IN   NEED
OF   LEADERSHIP:
TOMORROW'S   UNITED   NATIONS
- A   FRESH   APPRAISAL -

> ▸ coordination and improvement of the capacity of the **UN** system for development
>   cooperation;
> ▸ development of and respect for international law in its many new economic, environmental
>   and social, as well as its traditional spheres;
> ▸ promotion of respect for all human rights and their further codification, with particular
>   attention to eliminating discrimination based on gender;
> ▸ strengthening understanding of the value of cultural diversity and efforts to conserve it;
> ▸ the furtherance of basic and innovative research to support the above work, including
>   comprehensive global data banks and multidisciplinary analyses of global trends;
> ▸ stimulating participation in the **UN** system of all components of civil society: citizens and
>   their organizations, the business sector, research and academic institutions, and the
>   media.

Within this broad agenda, many specific problems make heavy demands on the leadership
capacity of the UN system. They are urgent problems whose interconnections require skilful
coordination of policies and programmes.

To take one example, massive poverty and ecological degradation in the South can only be
halted by better and more sustainable development; but this requires, among other things,
effective population planning, improved primary health care, better education and technical
training, changed agrarian policies, renewable energy sources to replace fuel-wood, and more
stable and favourable trade and financial arrangements for developing countries. These measures
in turn require, among other things, resolution of the debt problem and a return to a more stable
system of currencies and capital movements—at a time when market orientation in the North
encourages the reverse. Above all they require a new diversification of trading opportunities for
the 80 per cent of humanity who have only 19 per cent of world trade—at a time when North-
North trading systems are mushrooming. Ecological degradation in the North demands, at the
least, stringent and very costly anti-pollution measures. These measures coincide with
retrenchments in the defence industry and in other forms of employment. Such costs, together
with demands from Eastern Europe, have reduced North-South development cooperation which
is vital for the necessary sustainable development in the South.

The agenda for the 1990s that could be outlined at the beginning of the decade has been
widened and made more complex by political and cultural factors. The end of Cold War
constraints, the decline of central state power and of economies, and the new power of
communication, have unleashed old issues of national and ethnic identity long concealed across
imposed frontiers. History did not come to an end with the end of the Cold War; it began to table
countless long-neglected claims for resolution of problems from the age of empires.

The intricate economic and social problems often involved in such claims make their
energetic resolution the more urgent. Few have solely domestic remedies; many are actually
exacerbated by external actions like 'structural adjustment'. Trans-border communication of

ideas and news has made the world very volatile. It can encourage entire peoples to revolt. It also generates among the millions of the poor an ever-greater impatience, not only with their own elites but with international inequities.

A productive approach to such problems and to their inherent interconnections and contradictions calls for increasingly urgent analysis, the development of new ideas, and their active realization. The field of future potential action is vast. Only a continuous and tough-minded effort to define the issues that require global treatment, and those best handled regionally, will prevent a hopeless diffusion of resources and effort. Developing an active consensus about this world agenda and the UN system's part in it should be a central task for the Secretary-General and his or her colleagues in the UN system. Without this kind of leadership from the Secretary-General such a workable consensus for action is unlikely to emerge.

The agenda needs to be continuously subjected to decisions as to where the UN system can uniquely lead, promote and monitor; what its organizations can do and should be properly financed to do; and what they should *not* themselves do but where they can stimulate action, provide guidelines, and report to the world. In many instances North-South differences continue to be at the heart of this process and will require skilful, imaginative and coherent handling. There is at present no other group of more or less universal institutions in which these differences can be addressed comprehensively. It will, however, be impossible to carry out this task effectively until the work of the International Monetary Fund, the World Bank, and the World Trade Organization is conducted in harmony and coordination with the rest of the UN system.

Making a coherent and feasible strategy for the future; building intergovernmental consensus and engaging international public thinking in that consensus; strengthening and streamlining the UN system for its crucial roles; and initiating a serious programme of implementation at all levels; these are formidable tasks. They will need leadership at every level but, above all, imaginative and inspiring leadership from the United Nations.

III. THE SECRETARY-GENERAL

The first Secretary-General, Trygve Lie, described his as the most impossible job on earth. It would not be extravagant to describe it today as also the most important job on earth.

Aamir Ali in The Times of India, 16 July 1991

▶ Historical background

It is easy to say that the UN system needs strong, imaginative and independent leadership, but the reality is far more complex than that. Both governments and commentators have evinced considerable ambivalence on this subject down through the years, although in times of stress or expectation there has been a traditional tendency to dump sudden and unexpected tasks on the Secretary-General and his senior colleagues.

Ambiguities about the nature of the Secretary-Generalship have existed from the very outset. Even great power delegates at the founding UN Conference on International Organization in San Francisco acknowledged that the post could have an important political aspect; but in the end the UN Charter described the holder primarily as 'the chief administrative officer of the Organization', and sketched out far less clearly the political or coordinating functions of the post.

The Charter is even less forthcoming on qualifications for the post, stating merely that the Secretary-General and the staff 'shall not seek or receive instructions from any other authority external to the Organization. They shall refrain from any action which might reflect on their position as international officials responsible only to the Organization' (Article 100). Later on the Charter refers to the necessity of securing, in the Secretariat, the highest standards of efficiency, competence and integrity (Article 101).

In 1944 a group of former League of Nations officials made perhaps the most explicit, if sexist, attempt to describe the future Secretary-General's qualifications:

The qualities which the head of the service should possess are not easy to define. He should be young. Political or diplomatic experience, but not necessarily great fame or eminence, is an advantage. Above all, ability for administration in the broadest sense is important, implying a knowledge of when to be dynamic, to take the initiative and to force an issue; when, at the other extreme, to be content as a purely administrative official; and when, on a middle course, to be a moderator impartially smoothing over difficulties, a catalytic agent in negotiation.... In a new organization, it may well be that the only qualities which must under all conditions be demanded of the director are those of common sense, courage, integrity and tact.

The International Secretariat of the Future,
Royal Institute of International Affairs, London, March 1944

Before the appointment of the first Secretary-General, some delegations pondered on these matters without reaching very clear conclusions. A U.S. State Department meeting in August 1945 concluded that the future Secretary-General 'should be a man of recognized prestige and competence in the field of diplomacy and foreign office experience. He should be forty-five to fifty-five years of age and be fluent in both French and English... . It was generally agreed that it would be undesirable that the candidate should come from the USSR or from France.' A later memorandum widened the exclusions: 'The SG should, if possible, not be a national of one of the Big Five; he should be chosen because of his qualifications.' (The requisite qualifications were not stated.) In late September 1945, Adlai Stevenson told Edward R. Stettinius Jr., 'we favour choice of an outstandingly qualified individual, preferably a figure who has attained some international position and preferably a national of a small or middle power.'

A few specific names began to be mentioned. In late December 1945 when the appointment of the first Secretary-General was imminent, a State Department memo entitled 'Hot Topics expected to arise in the Assembly' noted that the appointment of the Secretary-General was the most important and urgent administrative matter and that 'a more common acceptance of the qualifications required for the SG would be helpful in arriving at a decision'. However, even two weeks before the appointment the State Department apparently had no candidate and no clear policy in mind, Alger Hiss noting to the Secretary of State on 19 January 1946 that 'the qualifications of the man should be the primary consideration' and that he should preferably not be a national of one of the five major powers. Trygve Lie, who began to be considered at a relatively late stage, was appointed on 1 February 1946.

In the prolonged search for a successor to Trygve Lie in late 1952 and early 1953, the name of Dag Hammarskjöld emerged at a late stage in the proceedings as a suggestion by the French Ambassador, who had been impressed by his work in Paris on the early stages of the Marshall Plan. Hammarskjöld himself was not consulted and was unaware that his name was being considered. He was virtually unknown to the other members of the Security Council, and was generally believed to be a non-political technocrat. Within less than two weeks he was Secretary-General.

Thereafter, whenever the post was about to become vacant, little consideration seems to have been given to the qualities or qualifications required of a future Secretary-General, nor indeed to the *need* for leadership qualities or to the demands which the forthcoming period in world affairs would be likely to make on the new leader.

Brian
Urquhart

Erskine
Childers

▶ What do Governments want?

> ... the rules of election aim at ensuring that the Secretary-General, as one of
> the main organs of the United Nations, shall have the opportunity of
> functioning as the spokesman of the Organization in its capacity as an
> independent opinion factor. This desire is natural and not particularly
> difficult to satisfy concerning administrative questions.... The problem is
> pointed up when the political and diplomatic responsibilities of the
> Secretary-General come into play.
>
> *Dag Hammarskjöld, 2 May 1959* [1]

Governments make this appointment, but what do governments really want from the Secretary-General? How do their attitudes while considering possible candidates correspond to what they expect of the Secretary-General once appointed?

Experience indicates that most governments want an adequate manager for the United Nations, a sympathetic ear for their concerns and complaints, and a person who can champion their cause in critical times. Since there are relatively few situations in which the objectives of all governments are the same (or, at least, will remain so), this last requirement creates many problems. That is why integrity and rugged independence are essential qualities for a Secretary-General. Governments tend to be nervous of too much political independence in the Secretary-General, especially if his or her views may turn out to be at variance with their policies on specific issues. This anxiety is nowhere more prevalent than among the five permanent members of the Security Council. The Prime Minister of one, asked by its Ambassador at the UN for instructions about an incumbent who was standing for a second term, cabled, 'We understand that he has not given us any trouble'. He was re-appointed.

To date, the industrial powers have tended to see the UN as a guardian of the *status quo* under pressure from developing countries, particularly in economic matters. Those more inclined to have the UN chart global solutions to economic and social problems have not argued this effectively with these governments. The developing world, containing the huge, impoverished majority of humankind has, on the other hand, been inclined to look to the UN as the potential agent of change.

The Secretary-General should be in a unique position to formulate and articulate truly global, mutually advantageous objectives in the economic and social fields and to convey their substance and importance to the media and the public as well as to governments. This, however, has not happened, and there is an increasingly dangerous vacuum in global leadership on critical economic and social problems.

Governments may also differ as to the relative importance of different aspects of the

---

[1]   In an address before the Student Association, Copenhagen, which he later described as a 'little handbook' concerning UN practices, UN history, and UN law 'which is handy for anybody who wants to form his own view regarding the possible role of the United Nations'.

Secretary-General's work—political, mediating, socio-economic, administrative, coordinating, generating new ideas, or communicating with the media and public opinion. Naturally governments do not wish either to be upstaged or publicly opposed, but they also need the Secretary-General to take initiatives in an emergency or when they themselves are unable to act.

Most governments regard the Secretary-General, in principle at any rate, as the guardian of the Charter. There are, however, frequent disagreements on the Charter's interpretation, and it has been a long time since an incumbent asserted an interpretation of the Charter against the opinion of a major power. Similarly there is general agreement on the Secretary-General's role as an intermediary in disputes between states, but precisely when or how is often a matter of controversy. Moreover, in the aftermath of the Cold War the role of the Secretary-General as mediator in a major crisis may be less indispensable.

On the other hand, the complexity and difficulty of the new generation of peace operations has greatly expanded the Secretary-General's responsibilities as an operational supervisor. In addition to these new dimensions, the gigantic humanitarian crises that now often accompany armed conflict require alert and sensitive leadership. When permanent members play active roles in peace-keeping operations, questions of command and control become more controversial. The post-Cold War possibility of using regional military organizations like NATO in pursuit of Security Council objectives may radically affect the role of the Secretary-General in matters of peace and security. The partial use of force in some operations has also complicated the Secretary-General's classic role of impartial intermediary and negotiator.

▶ What do the people want?

The strength and endurance of the United Nations will ultimately depend to a large extent on its public support in member countries. Certainly the perception of the UN as an often helpless agent between the Cold War giants led to a severe reduction of the original vision and an indifference to and ignorance of the world organization, especially in the Western world. The recent surge of interest in the UN among the non-governmental organizations (NGOs) that are mushrooming in so many fields of UN endeavour, and the general world-wide restiveness of citizens, may augur an end to such indifference, but only if the UN can prove itself effective in the tasks that are assigned to it.

> The Big Five, if left to make the decision in secret conclave, are likely to reach down to the lowest common denominator, (not) repeating the mistake of picking another Hammarskjöld. The only force that could persuade them to accept an outstanding person is the pressure exercised by media attention and an informed public opinion.
> *Max Jakobson, World Monitor, August 1991*[2]

---

[2] Max Jakobson, Finland's Ambassador to the UN from 1965 to 1972, was one of the candidates for Secretary-General in 1971.

Brian
Urquhart

Erskine
Childers

*A   WORLD   IN   NEED
OF   LEADERSHIP:
TOMORROW'S   UNITED   NATIONS
- A   FRESH   APPRAISAL -*

Surrounded at UN world conferences by anything up to 30,000 NGO people from all corners of the globe, governments are becoming aware that the UN is no longer their exclusive preserve. Indeed the public, and at least parts of the media, seem to be beginning to see the United Nations as the public service sector of a world community that does not yet exist but that they would wish to see developed.

Will governments be prepared to pay more serious attention to what 'We, the Peoples', who open the Charter, actually want the United Nations to be, and therefore to what they expect of the Secretary-General? A wise and careful but charismatic, fearless and articulate champion of peace, justice, law, human rights and reason would certainly attract widespread popular support in today's confused and violent world. Such a person would not necessarily make all governments happy, but those most ardently professing devotion to democracy and the will of the people might do well to consider what sort of person the peoples of the world would actually wish to see in the Secretary-General's post.

▶ *Problems of coherence and coordination in the UN system*

> The capability of the UN system to make comprehensive reviews of the
> functioning of the world economy and the prospects for development
> must be strengthened and made credible.
>
> *The South Commission, 1990*[3]

The Secretary-General has always been expected to provide a focal point and a sense of direction in complex international dealings. As indicated earlier, however, there has so far been little emphasis on the UN providing intellectual leadership to shape a global economic and social agenda and encourage cooperative action to realise it. In a reinvigorated United Nations system this should become a central part of the Secretary-General's role.

The international community is more and more dangerously divided on North-South lines. While there is enthusiasm in Northern quarters for 'globalization' and the market, the evidence steadily increases that, whatever benefits they may bring to some, alleviating mass poverty is not among them. Indeed in most places globalization and the market have brought the reverse.

Leading figures in the private sector are themselves expressing anxiety. Restoring a due measure of representative intergovernmental management to a world economy which is in effect an interdependent one of 6 billion people will become increasingly necessary. If stability is perceived to be vital for everyone's future, wise and disinterested global approaches will be indispensable.

---

[3] *The Challenge to the South*, Report of the South Commission (Oxford University Press, 1990), page 225.

As in each agency, there is also a need for a high-level centre of leadership
for the UN system as a whole with the capacity to assess, advise, assist and
report on the progress made and needed for sustainable development.
That leadership should be provided by the Secretary-General of the
United Nations Organization.

The Brundtland Report, Our Common Future [4]

The role of the Secretary-General in diplomacy, conflict-resolution and peace-keeping has
hitherto dominated the consideration of candidates for the post. With this role's connotation of
reticence and detachment, can the same person also be manager of the global agenda, public
educator on international economic and social issues, and advocate of law and human rights? The
answer henceforth has to be Yes, but clearly with the necessary organizational changes. The
working relations of the central United Nations organization with the system of specialized
agencies, funds and programmes are also an important, though sometimes neglected, part of the
Secretary-General's functions.

Although its political and security functions usually attract the most media attention, the
UN system is concerned with virtually all fields of human activity and need. Surprisingly,
however, it has for the most part not been used as a system by governments over the years.

As we have pointed out in *Renewing the United Nations System* (Dag Hammarskjöld
Foundation, 1994), the decision of the first General Assembly that the headquarters of the
specialized agencies should be located at the same site as the UN itself has never been
implemented. Ever since, sectoral Ministers meet and speak only to each other in Washington,
Rome, Paris, Geneva and other agency headquarters, while foreign office diplomats talk to each
other in New York. Failure to complete the intended architecture of the UN system has been
compounded by major powers steadily drawing the International Monetary Fund and World
Bank (and now the new World Trade Organization) away from the UN, while weakening the
UN's economic policy formulation capacity.

Given these problems, it is not surprising that the Economic and Social Council (ECOSOC)
has never successfully performed the strategy-negotiating and coordinating functions which the
Charter assigned to it in relation to the whole system, including the Bretton Woods institutions.
This does not mean that ECOSOC needs to be replaced; it means that all governments must agree
to implement its Charter role. They must also begin to coordinate their own policies in the
different parts of the UN system. Some regularly call for strong, multidisciplinary coordination
in the United Nations, but allow for—and even stimulate—the reverse in the governing bodies of
the specialized agencies.

The Secretary-General has at present no power to coordinate this fractured system
effectively. He does not have the outright authority to direct its specialized agency heads. He

---

[4]   World Commission on Environment and Development, *Our Common Future* (Oxford University Press, 1987),
    page 318.

Brian
Urquhart

Erskine
Childers

A   W O R L D   I N   N E E D
O F   L E A D E R S H I P :
T O M O R R O W ' S   U N I T E D   N A T I O N S
- A   F R E S H   A P P R A I S A L -

cannot ensure a proper division of effort. Inevitably there is a lack of integrated intellectual analysis to animate the activities of the whole system. Effective UN performance depends on a radical improvement in the working relationships of the different parts of the system. Measures are needed to ensure that the heads of the key agencies will in future join the Secretary-General to form what would, in effect, be an international cabinet for an energetic, coordinated approach to global problems. In the second section of this study we outline ways of adjusting the system which we detailed in our 1994 study. Authoritative leadership by the Secretary-General would be vital to their success.

▶ The scope of the job and qualities needed

> For some one whose job so obviously mirrors man's extraordinary
> possibilities and responsibilities, there is no excuse if he loses his sense of
> 'having been called'. So long as he keeps that, everything he can do has a
> meaning, nothing a price. Therefore: if he complains, he is accusing—
> himself.
>
> *Dag Hammarskjöld in Markings , 23 June 1957* [5]

In the post-Cold War period the dramas and complexities of expanded peace-keeping operations have dominated the world's perception of the United Nations. The other, more long-term work of the organization (not least, addressing underlying causes of conflict) is not any less important in the agenda of the Secretary-General, but it tends to be obscured by the more sensational aspects of peace-keeping operations. Resolution of the world's economic, social, and ecological problems is increasingly an indispensable complement of peace and security. If anything, these aspects of the Secretary-General's duties, and those of his senior colleagues in the Secretariat and the specialized agencies have assumed even greater importance.

Co-ordination and management of the system will be more and more vital to future effectiveness. To the traditionally perceived duties of the Secretary-General as a diplomat, mediator, and administrator must now be added the duties of team leader and *animateur*, with the capacity to conceptualize, organize, delegate and coordinate international work over a vast range of human activity. He or she must be able to mobilize the intellectual and organizational resources for this task.

If the work is to be effective, the Secretary-General must also look beyond the purely intergovernmental sphere to the community at large, and to non-governmental agencies and organizations. For many of the key items of the international agenda—human rights, the status of women, or the environment, for example—much of the necessary dynamism and capacity to get

---

[5]   Hammarskjöld began keeping a diary-book 'concerning my negotiations with myself and with God' when he was 20. From the day he was told of his appointment to be Secretary-General he entered the date of each of his 'markings'. He left the manuscript to be published after his death. (New York, Knopf, 1964), page 132.

intergovernmental decisions into action will come increasingly from these sources. The Secretary-General must also be sensitive to the will and concerns of the public. Indeed, the UN's machinery must eventually include a standing forum for the voices of the people to be heard.[6]

The responsibilities of the Secretary-General are constantly expanding, and the job currently comprises a number of more or less full-time jobs. These include:

▸ administering and managing a global organization and a world-wide staff on a shoestring budget, a sizable part of which is usually overdue;
▸ implementing the decisions of the General Assembly, the Security Council, the Economic and Social Council, and other UN bodies;
▸ running peace-keeping and other highly sensitive operations;
▸ being the intermediary in an open-ended series of disputes and disagreements all over the world;
▸ providing good offices in human rights and humanitarian situations;
▸ generating ideas and strategies on global problems;
▸ co-ordinating the UN system of specialized agencies and major economic and social programmes;
▸ representing the United Nations worldwide at global and regional conferences, and to the media and public;
▸ maintaining a global watch on major developments of all kinds and alerting governments to them.

Obviously the Secretary-General can only hope to perform these tasks adequately through a well thought out delegation of some functions, which should also bring a new synergy to the discharge of all of them. Still, however, the question needs to be asked and answered, how can all this be handled by one person?

The answer involves, first, a careful distinction between qualities and qualifications. Different Secretaries-General have tackled their tasks in different ways, but the *qualities* that are unquestionably required are not difficult to list.

▸ stature, integrity and moral courage
▸ resistance to untoward pressures
▸ commitment to social justice, democratic values
▸ diplomatic skill combined with a world view
▸ respect for cultural diversity
▸ fair-mindedness and freedom from cynicism
▸ maturity of character and absence of excessive ego
▸ executive ability and ability to choose the best deputies and to delegate authority
▸ broad intellectual background and discipline
▸ analytical capability and insight

---

[6] We have recommended in our 1994 study early work to develop an elected United Nations Parliamentary Assembly alongside the General Assembly of governments.

Brian
Urquhart

Erskine
Childers

A   W O R L D   I N   N E E D
O F   L E A D E R S H I P :
T O M O R R O W ' S   U N I T E D   N A T I O N S
– A   F R E S H   A P P R A I S A L –

▸   ability to develop and pursue original ideas
▸   ability to communicate ideas and to inspire people in the world at large
▸   physical stamina
▸   a sense of proportion and humour

It must be emphasised that none of these are 'qualifications'. They are personal qualities and attributes which can be found in one individual. The world's chief public servant *should* be a most unusual person.

A Secretary-General with the *qualities* noted above could handle the job as *the leader of a team* of rigorously selected and highly qualified deputies and, in a second larger circle, as the accepted and respected leader of the larger team of heads of the UN system as a whole. Such a leader must also be able to inspire the international civil service and ensure it is brought to the highest standards of capability, performance, and personal integrity. The end of the East-West ideological struggle frees a Secretary-General to work far more effectively in all fields of activity through a managed delegation of authority.

> No Secretary-General can afford to lose a sense of obligation to the human
> community in its broadest sense.
>
> *Secretary-General U Thant* [7]

An extraordinary range of intellect and perception is critically important in enabling a Secretary-General to be a public advocate and a team leader in so many fields, and to command the intellectual respect of senior colleagues. This is not an impossible profile either. Until the age of specialization the encyclopaedic mind was regarded with greatest respect in all cultures. The Secretary-General of the United Nations needs to possess such a mind and outlook. It is not impossible to find.

If governments held the foregoing picture clearly in mind as they approached the selection of a Secretary-General there would, first of all, be a new interest in ensuring a higher-quality senior echelon around the Secretary-General. In our 1994 study we recommended that the Secretary-General's top team comprise four Deputy Secretaries-General: for political, security and peace affairs; international economic co-operation and sustainable development; humanitarian affairs; and administration, management and conference services (the High Commissioner for Human Rights should also have Deputy rank). These Deputies should be of rank higher than any executive head in the UN system. A system of deputies would allow for a reduction of the present large top echelon of officials. *This echelon structure and rank should be decided by the General Assembly, leaving its implementation to the new Secretary-General.* This matter is further discussed in the second section of this study.

Another result of keeping this profile in mind would be the need to select as Secretary-

---

  [7]   Speaking to the United Nations Correspondents Association (UNCA), 16 September 1971, New York.

General a person who would be able to lead and work with a multidisciplinary team of top-calibre people. An ability to select such a team and to lead it, including readiness to delegate authority and to share the limelight would be essential. Governments, of course, would also have to be willing to deal with deputies on day-to-day matters.

Undertaking an energetic and well-organized search across the world for such a truly outstanding Secretary-General, governments would not merely wait until aspirants to the office appear—usually from a narrow reservoir of familiar names, quite literally the 'old boy network'. Nor would they restrict themselves to diplomats or politicians, but rather initiate a worldwide search for candidates with the *qualities* listed above.

We may be considered naive in putting forward this rather high-minded suggestion for the selection process. We are prompted to do so, however, not only by the very great potential importance of the job, but also by the undeniable fact that appointing the Secretary-General has to date been a curiously haphazard and to some extent lowest common denominator affair. The actual selection has been the product of chance more than of a deliberate search for the best, or of foresight, consultation, or planning at the highest levels of government.

We wrote in 1990: 'It might be said to be remarkable, with such a method of selection, that the results have been, on the whole, as good as they have.' It must be questioned more than ever whether the present procedure is remotely adequate for such an important appointment.

IV. THE SELECTION PROCESS 1945-1991

Certain unwritten and purely informal assumptions about the Secretary-Generalship have grown up. The Secretary-General should serve a five-year renewable term of office. The Secretary-General should not be a national of one of the five Permanent Members of the Security Council. The veto applies to the Security Council's recommendation. Governments alone are responsible for the selection and recommendation process.

Other assumptions have been vaguer. The Secretary-Generalship should in theory rotate among geographical regions. The background of candidates should be diplomatic or political. The Secretary-General shall be a man. The candidates seriously considered have all, hitherto, been men.

A study of how the six Secretaries-General since 1946 were appointed creates two main impressions—the last-minute and poorly prepared nature of the process, and the lack of determination to find a superlative candidate for the job.

▶ *Who appoints?*

At Dumbarton Oaks the idea that the Secretary-General be elected directly by the General Assembly was strongly opposed by the great powers who were to be the permanent members of the Security Council. A subsequent proposal that the Security Council should make the recommendation by a majority of seven votes (the Council originally had eleven members), but that the veto power of the permanent members should not be applicable, was also strongly resisted by the permanent members. The argument was that the election of the Secretary-General was not a procedural matter.

The issue was debated again at San Francisco. Amendments were offered by Australia, Egypt, Honduras, Mexico, Uruguay and Venezuela to lessen the control of the Security Council over the selection of the Secretary-General. Mexico, for example, proposed nomination by a majority of the Council; Belgium and Canada urged that the Security Council vote need not include the affirmative vote of the permanent members. This was rejected by the United States. The Netherlands made forceful arguments against the applicability of the veto and suggested that if the veto applied to the selection, then re-election should not be allowed.

The permanent members again argued that this was a substantive matter, and that in any case the Secretary-General would need the support of the major powers to do his job.

These and other arguments did not move the permanent members, and, despite lengthy debate, it had to be accepted that the veto *would* apply to the appointment of the Secretary-General. Article 97 of the Charter states that 'The Secretary-General shall be appointed by the General Assembly upon the recommendation of the Security Council'. As one ambassador pointed out, the word 'electing' would have given the General Assembly the authority to choose a candidate, but in 'appointing' it could only confirm or reject.

Australia, Belgium, Canada and the Netherlands took the view that the application of the veto might impair the independence of action of the Secretary-General. The Netherlands also maintained that the application of the veto by one of the permanent members,

would compel the permanent members to reach a compromise, and this might result in the appointment of a 'lowest common denominator'. Furthermore the Secretary-General would work in the knowledge that his chances of re-election would be small if he were to incur the displeasure of one of the permanent members.

▶ Who starts the process?

It is a normal requirement in top appointments to publicly accountable institutions that on a certain date there is a call for nominations and a closing date is prescribed for their submission. Not even this minimal procedure exists for the Secretary-Generalship of the United Nations. As Table 5 shows (page 46), in these as in other respects many agencies of the UN system have more disciplined and deliberate procedures for nomination of their executive heads than does the system's central organization.

> ... a process as arcane as it is ritualistic, perhaps best compared with
> appointments of the British judiciary, in that they 'emerge' as if by magic.
> *Sarah Helm, The Independent, 18 September 1991*

No official or body initiates the nomination of candidates for Secretary-General. Candidates usually just proclaim themselves, or are put forward by their governments. Not even a single-page biography is required, and no body verifies, on behalf of the UN's member states, the assertions about their record made by candidates themselves.

Certainly the permanent missions at United Nations Headquarters exchange views and gossip on the matter, and keep their capitals informed. Foreign Offices with active United Nations desks take an interest and eventually decide at least which candidates are unacceptable, and even which candidates they most favour. There has, however, for many years been remarkably little evidence of serious discussion of the Secretary-Generalship at higher levels of government, and even less of a dispassionate high-level consideration of the nature of the task or of the qualities, background and expertise required to provide the best future leadership. Indeed some important governments do not seem to think of the Secretary-General as a leader at all (except when for their own reasons they decide he should be).

Brian
Urquhart

Erskine
Childers

*A WORLD IN NEED
OF LEADERSHIP:
TOMORROW'S UNITED NATIONS
- A FRESH APPRAISAL -*

▶ The role of the veto

The veto power in the Security Council has remained a decisive factor in the selection of the Secretary-General, an eliminating process before the Security Council makes its recommendation to the General Assembly. Between 1945-1990 permanent members vetoed candidates 43 times (15 per cent of all vetoes), and many more times by one or more merely making known their disapproval of a candidate (sometimes called 'a shadow veto'). The essential choice of the Secretary-General has thus in practice been made by the five permanent members, and the decision of the General Assembly has been more or less a rubber-stamp.

This has inescapable implications. Five governments have arrogated to themselves the major responsibility for who will be the Secretary-General of the United Nations. One might suppose that they would exercise exceptional care and diligence in discharging this exceptional responsibility. So far, however, this does not appear to have been the case. After fifty years and the end of the Cold War, there seems no compelling reason why the permanent members should not *relinquish* the veto for this crucial process. The first permanent member to do so would be acclaimed by the world.

> ... months slid by with little sense of urgency about choosing a leader for
> the next five and possibly 10 years ...
>
> *Time, December 2, 1991*

▶ The role of the General Assembly

The General Assembly's function in appointing the Secretary-General has been made even more of a rubber-stamp by the lack of a proper timetable for the total process. The Security Council is under no obligation as to when it shall send its recommendation to the General Assembly, except presumably that it should do so before the current Secretary-General's term actually expires. In instances where a new Secretary-General was definitely to be appointed, Council members have shown some concern to make their recommendation in time for a reasonable transition. This, however, has been more for the benefit of the selected candidate than for those who are actually to appoint him. Even such limited concern can evaporate in the confusion of secret manoeuvring.

The sense of all other (now 180) delegations that they are merely waiting for the final word to emanate from the 'permanent five' creates an atmosphere in which it has seemed indecorous for *the actual appointment body* to do anything except convene and forthwith approve. In the appointment of the first Secretary-General, and to one degree or another in all subsequent ones, there has not been adequate time for the membership as a whole to give full consideration to its actual responsibility of approving or rejecting the recommendation of the Security Council. The General Assembly has theoretically always had the power to refuse a Security Council recommendation but this has not, so far, played any significant part in the process.

The General Assembly should adopt a timetable for the entire procedure, including a cutoff date by which the Council must submit its recommendation. The General Assembly should be ready properly to review and, if its majority so judges, to reject a recommendation from the Council that the membership as a whole deems inadequate.

► Campaigning

> Most candidates are non-candidates, or non-non candidates, depending on
> the degree of sublimation of their candidacies.
>
> John Newhouse, The New Yorker, December 16, 1991

The practice of candidates campaigning for the office of Secretary-General emerged around 1970. It has further confused and downgraded an already disoriented and unsystematic process, while also favouring those with means to travel and promote themselves.

Right from the beginning, unless they were running a candidate themselves, governments seem to have considered the selection of a new Secretary-General only when names had begun to emerge and lobbying by self-proclaimed candidates had already begun. The process then became a matter of examining the field, picking possible winners, deciding who had to be blocked, discarding unsuitable candidates, and bargaining for either the best available among them, or the least bad. Latterly, discussions in regional groups have sometimes played a part in putting together bloc support for a particular candidate. The knowledge that the veto would, in the end, determine the outcome seems for the most part to have discouraged an imaginative approach to the matter, based on a wide-ranging search procedure.

► Term of office

The re-eligibility of an incumbent Secretary-General, or the obvious wish of an incumbent to stay on, has also repeatedly affected the appointment process, and should therefore be reviewed at this point.

The Charter is mute about the important questions of length of term and re-election. A term of three years had been recommended both in the Dumbarton Oaks proposal and at San Francisco where the term length was a matter of some debate (Mexico proposed a single 7-10-year term). The subsequent Preparatory Commission recommended five years to the first, 1946 General Assembly. Resolution 11(I) of 24 January 1946 stated, 'the first Secretary-General shall be appointed for five years, the appointment being open at the end of that period for a further five-year term'. Clearly applying only to the first Secretary-General to allow him to follow through with the start-up of the organization, the resolution added, 'there being no stipulation on the subject in the Charter, the General Assembly and the Security Council are free to modify the term of office of future Secretaries-General in the light of experience'. Charles Weitz has reviewed in detail the recurring debates on length and renewability of term in FAO for its Director-General.

Brian
Urquhart

Erskine
Childers

*A   WORLD   IN   NEED
OF   LEADERSHIP :
TOMORROW'S   UNITED   NATIONS
- A   FRESH   APPRAISAL -*

By curious contrast, in the United Nations there has been no serious debate for fifty years on the merits of the five-year, renewable term. It has merely become the accepted practice, one of various assumptions about the post that have never been seriously re-examined.

There is nothing sacrosanct about this assumption. Its disadvantages have been pointed out many times. The job is so demanding, and so physically and mentally strenuous, that ten years may be too long. On the other hand five years is a relatively short time to initiate and carry through important policies or reforms.

As regards re-eligibility, an incumbent Secretary-General clearly desiring to be reappointed may be subjected to undesirable pressures; some have been, and some have yielded to them. The tradition of reappointment, abetted by the natural aversion of governments to change and their reluctance to face making a new choice, can lead to staleness. Here again the absence of any rules for the top UN post has its effect. For example, an incumbent need not indicate his intentions until virtually the last days of his term. This leaves the diplomatic community, ever concerned about diplomatic manners, apprehensive about even discussing a future appointment, let alone engaging in an adequate search procedure.

> Effective as of the next election, Secretaries-General should be elected for a
> single term not to exceed seven years.
> *A Successor Vision: The United Nations of Tomorrow* [8]

In the light of these and other considerations discussed later in this study, *a single term of seven years* would have many advantages. It would give a Secretary-General the opportunity to undertake far-reaching plans, free from undesirable pressures. It would make possible a more orderly and considered process for selecting the best possible successor. In our view the seven-year, single term of office is the key to improving the whole appointment process. It should be established as soon as possible.

▶ *The nature of the process*

From the foregoing it emerges that the process (if indeed it can be called such) for the appointment of the Secretary-General has so far been largely confined to *a disorderly procedure to secure a nomination.* There has been little or no methodical search to find candidates outstandingly equipped for an important and extraordinarily difficult job. Rather, the basic criterion appears to have been to find a reasonably acceptable candidate who could get past all five potential vetoes.

As already mentioned, the appointment has tended to become more and more quite literally an 'old-boy network' affair. It is only natural that permanent representatives to the UN, with their admirable collegial tradition, should tend to be predisposed in favour of candidates known to

---

[8]   The report of an international panel assembled by the United Nations Association of the USA, 1988, page 204.

them who are in one way or another part of the diplomatic scene. But this has also limited both the field of candidates considered and the breadth of their outlook and experience. It has led on one occasion to a serious case of inadequate record-checking; on another, to ignoring past diplomatic activities that on occasion hampered an incumbent's effectiveness; and on more than one occasion to ignoring evidence of excessive egocentricity, with serious consequences for the running of the UN.

The search for the best possible Secretary-General *demands* a more effective effort by member governments. It is therefore worth reviewing some other aspects of the problem.

▶ Regional rotation

A secondary criterion after the veto has been a notion of rotating the post among the main geographical regions. Finding the best in the world has never been an unqualified objective. Regional rotation is a customary procedure for other UN offices (presidents of organs, etc.).

This approach to the office may be less used in the future. Meanwhile it is vital to observe that it is not in itself inconsistent with finding the best possible candidate.

▶ '... the equal rights of men and women ...'

No woman has to date even been a candidate for Secretary-General of a United Nations whose Charter explicitly commits it to the equality of women and men both in its Preamble and in a specific Article (8). Somewhat more than half of 'We, the Peoples of the United Nations' have not even been considered as a source for the post. This is grotesque, and profoundly damaging. The kind of search which we recommend in this study should deliberately include seeking truly outstanding women. It would be very healthy for the international community if one of them were to be its next Secretary-General.

▶ Candidates from Permanent Members

Until now, there has been a general feeling that political conditions made it unwise to reconsider the tradition that a national of a permanent member country cannot be a candidate for Secretary-General. In 1990 we observed that, since this exclusion is related to the veto power over candidatures on which permanent members had always insisted, a trade-off between the two might be considered.

Certainly, *any* exclusion by nationality is incompatible with the concept of finding the best possible world figure capable of gaining the confidence of all parts of the international community. The willingness of the international community to lift the exclusion of the nationals of permanent members may in large part depend on the willingness of the permanent members to relinquish the veto over the recommendation of a Secretary-General.

31

Brian
Urquhart

Erskine
Childers

A WORLD IN NEED
OF LEADERSHIP:
TOMORROW'S UNITED NATIONS
- A FRESH APPRAISAL -

▶ A diplomatic yet democratic selection?

There remain some dilemmas. Campaigning is manifestly undesirable; but so would be a wholly secretive process of selection dominated by major powers, even with a search process. Public institutions, non-governmental organizations and media should contribute their ideas for the best candidate. All UN-member governments should have a similar opportunity, and not merely have to wait to accept or reject a single candidate finally recommended by the Security Council. These dilemmas could be resolved. The objective is to develop a search and selection process by governments which casts as wide a net as possible and which can engage the interest and contribution of the broader public in this intergovernmental process.

The commencement of a new selection process should be formally announced no later than 1 January of the appointment year by the President of the General Assembly as appointing body. The announcement should invite governments, parliaments, non-governmental institutions and individuals to send suggestions to the President of the Security Council by a specific date.

From a properly scheduled and thorough search, including any such relevant suggestions, the Security Council should, by mid-year, distil a short list of not less than 5, not more than 10 candidates. This list should be publicly released and distributed world-wide, inviting comment and possible alternative names from governments and parliamentarians and the public. After four weeks this open scrutiny would end and the Security Council would resume its effort to produce a single recommendation.

This two-stage public involvement would, we believe, resolve many dilemmas. It would make possible both governmental and public suggestions at the outset, and allow for the scrutiny of the selection process at mid-point, with a further chance for comment and suggestion. It would involve all member governments at a stage much earlier than the point at which the General Assembly must accept or reject a single nominee.

The suggested procedure would, of course, entail considerably more work (and no doubt some silly nominations as well, but the present procedure also attracts these). The total timetable for such a process would undoubtedly have to commence no later than 1 January of the appointment year, and the search group would have to be operational on that date, and very efficiently managed. Many small national institutions take more time and trouble than this to find a new head. Finding the kind of Secretary-General the international community needs certainly deserves nothing less.

We have assembled this analysis and set out these proposals in full knowledge that the political aspects of the matter cannot be ignored, and also that the procedures of the United Nations inevitably involve lobbying and bargaining. Governments, not to mention candidates, would have to accept scrutiny, expert advice and wider canvassing of possible candidates. We can find no convincing argument why they should not accept procedures which are considered both normal and essential in great enterprises elsewhere. We are convinced that the present process *can* be improved, and that the conditions of our changing world demand it.

▶ *An improved process*

The suggested improvements can be summarised as follows:

1. As the highest policy-making organ of the United Nations and as the ultimate appointing body, the General Assembly should adopt a comprehensive resolution establishing a single seven-year term and all key features of an improved process of appointing the Secretary-General. With adoption of a seven-year single term such matters could be discussed in the General Assembly without embarrassment to the incumbent Secretary-General.

2. If the General Assembly decision is too close to the expiration of the present term the incumbent could be invited to accept a short extension.

3. The essential elements of an improved process are:

   ► serious consideration by governments of the necessary qualifications for the post in light of world conditions and probable future demands on the UN;

   ► a single seven-year term;

   ► an internationally publicised announcement of the commencement of the selection procedure and a call for nominations;

   ► internationally publicized rules and timetable for nominations and the minimal required documentation;

   ► a mechanism for checking records and assessing qualities, background, etc.;

   ► a timetable that fully allows for a proper worldwide search, refinement of a list of candidates, four weeks of public exposure of this short list, and for the General Assembly to fulfil its responsibilities;

   ► a well organized search for the best qualified candidates worldwide, not excluding but giving no undue significance to self-nominated or nationally sponsored candidates;

   ► the inclusion of women candidates in the search;

   ► the cessation of the practice of individual campaigning for the Secretary-Generalship which will be considered disqualifying behaviour;

   ► a process for contribution of suggestions for the office by all governments, parliaments and the public and for their comments on the short list from the first stage of Security Council search;

   ► a full and transparent accounting by the Security Council of its discharge of its responsibilities in the selection including record of all informal and formal votes.

4. The search group, to be established by and to report to the Security Council, should be representative of the Council's non-permanent and permanent members. It should be authorized and provided with resources to seek information and advice from any source, including the non-governmental community. Its work before and after the mid-point public listing should be carried out in the strictest confidentiality.

5. The search group would examine the qualifications and background of all nominees, with the option to interview them and, if necessary, to conduct a wider search again for candidates. It should consult with the regional groups.

Brian
Urquhart

Erskine
Childers

A   W O R L D   I N   N E E D
O F   L E A D E R S H I P :
T O M O R R O W ' S   U N I T E D   N A T I O N S
– A   F R E S H   A P P R A I S A L –

The aim of such arrangements would be to produce a broader and better choice of candidates, to avoid a desperate last-minute search for a compromise candidate, and to give more weight to the views of all member governments, and the public worldwide.

It will be argued by some that the above suggestions constitute a complicated alternative to a relatively casual process which on balance has not worked too badly in the past, and that they will only cause unnecessary work, trouble, and even embarrassment to potential candidates. However, no serious assessment of the overall history of the post of Secretary-General could lead to the conclusion that the present manner of selection has been adequate. It has not.

V. CONCLUSIONS

The world will not simply run itself in a safe, equitable manner. The era of imperial powers is ending. The need for well-directed international cooperation that commands the confidence of nations large and small increases week by week. This demands the best possible leadership for the United Nations system, the only existing universal framework for intergovernmental cooperation and international management.

This is a testing time for the United Nations. It is a time when the urgent need for international action is confronted by coalitions of powerful special interests and potentially explosive restiveness in many parts of this fragile world, as well as outspoken ideological opposition to international organization. It is a time when the balance between national sovereignty and international responsibility has constantly to be adjusted. It is a time when wise transnational leadership is vital for human well-being—perhaps even for human survival.

The UN system faces two broad tasks, to combine peace-keeping and peace-making in a more consistent, representative and reliable framework for international peace and security, and to find the best way to deal equitably with the causes of upheaval and conflict and the major issues of global interdependence. Inspired and skilful leadership is needed to mobilize the UN system to its full potential. Essential international objectives and programmes have to be imaginatively shaped and persuasively presented to the public and to governments. They then have to be implemented efficiently and effectively.

These are formidable tasks for the Secretary-General and his or her colleagues who run the different parts of the system. Only if they become a team, working towards the same goals on an agreed plan with the full support of governments, can they hope to succeed.

The question of leadership is obviously not the whole answer. It cannot be separated from the necessity for governments to adapt the UN system to the pressing realities of our times. Leadership will also be a part of that process and will be vital to its success.

The appointed leadership of the United Nations functions, of course, within the realities of the existing power structures of world politics. Although these are less assertive than before there are residual limitations to what even the most inspired and courageous international leadership can achieve.

The best selection procedures will, however, be useless without the will and the sustained interest of governments in making them work. Obviously there is no perfect or infallible system, but the risks can be greatly reduced by a stronger emphasis on the main objective, finding the best candidate for the job. None of the suggestions that are made in this study would require any change in the United Nations Charter, or in any other basic documents of the system.

The Secretary-General of the United Nations will, in reality, usually suffer from crushing responsibilities without significant power and resources, and from the contrary attitudes of

Brian
Urquhart

Erskine
Childers

A   WORLD   IN   NEED
OF   LEADERSHIP:
TOMORROW'S   UNITED   NATIONS
– A   FRESH   APPRAISAL –

governments as well as often unrealistic public expectations. These natural obstacles can be overcome only by a personality both authoritative and charismatic, by a visionary determination and dedication to the creative evolution of international institutions. Such a person must also be motivated by a deep-seated conviction that the nations and peoples now face obstacles which can only be overcome through cooperation and sustained effort, an effort that will be literally vital to the future of humankind.

CHAPTER TWO

A SYSTEM IN NEED OF LEADERSHIP

I. INTRODUCTION

> The behaviour of executive heads of the UN system would be transformed
> if we had Hammarskjölds, *always*, as Secretary-General.
>
> *Halfdan Mahler* [9]

The Secretary-General is the leader of the United Nations itself and, in a second dimension, the leader of leaders in the UN system of specialized agencies and funds.[10] The lack of attention to the capacity for inter-disciplinary leadership needed in a Secretary-General has already been noted. Apart from that, governments have seldom considered readiness to work in a team as a requirement for heads of agencies and funds. In his study of FAO elections Charles Weitz observes that the problems are circular: the best possible leadership for the different parts of the system is unlikely to be achieved without policy-initiatives by member-states for the system as a whole. Those initiatives will have to come from its centre, the UN itself.

Finding leadership of high competence and integrity in public service is not an exact science. The recommendations made in this study could not by themselves guarantee the kind and quality of UN-system leadership that the world needs. The realistic question is: what improvements in the process would provide a better chance of finding the most effective people and team?

Only governments, however, and those who advise governments, can effectively improve the process. Improvement in rules and procedures alone will not secure the desired results if those who make the decisions and who influence decision-makers are not seriously interested in strengthening the United Nations and its system. If they are so concerned, rules and procedures can make possible a better process of search and selection, and can perhaps reduce the chances of, or the damage from, serious mistakes.

This chapter, therefore, after a survey of basic problems, examines in greater depth all the selection processes of the UN system. It draws especially on the Weitz study of FAO elections because experience in that major Specialized Agency mirrors problems elsewhere in the system.

---

[9]   Former Director-General of the World Health Organization (WHO), speaking at a conference on the International Health System, April 1996, Uppsala.

[10] 'Specialized Agencies', hereafter called 'the agencies', are separately established international organizations brought into special relationship with the United Nations under Charter Articles 57 and 63. They are listed, beginning with ILO, in the UN system diagram on page 6. The 'funds' referred to are special UN funds and programmes for development cooperation and humanitarian purposes, like UNDP and UNICEF, largely financed by voluntary contributions, established by the General Assembly and officially directed by the Secretary-General who appoints their executive heads. They are listed in the left-hand column of the same diagram.

II. THE SALIENT PROBLEMS

> Until governments find mechanisms to develop comprehensive policy for
> leadership in the UN system, and ensure consistent application of that
> policy, there is less likelihood of finding the optimum direction for FAO.
> *Charles H. Weitz , Who Speaks for the Hungry* [11]

From the outset a certain ambivalence has characterized the relationship between the centre and
the surrounding organizations of the evolving United Nations system. The responsibility for this
is broadly shared.

Most Secretaries-General have soon wearied of attempts to guide the system through the
Administrative Committee on Co-ordination, perhaps not least because most of them lacked any
profound interest in the economic, social and technological work of their colleagues to begin
with.[12] For their part, many agency heads have taken advantage of this lack of interest at the
centre and have gone their own ways. The most effective heads have, however, deplored the
absence of dynamic leadership from the UN.

At the intergovernmental level the same states that are members of the various
organizations frequently call, in the UN itself, for 'system-wide co-ordination', while speaking to
the contrary in agency councils.

This contradiction, and its underlying cause in the constitutional separateness of the
system's parts, inhibits coherent action by governments over leadership in the system. Other than
watching broadly over regional balances in the total list of executive heads, there is no common
approach to this crucial problem.

▶ Selection in the Specialized Agencies

Although no common policy exists regarding leadership of the Specialized Agencies, their
procedures for the appointment of their chief officers appear more systematic and explicit than
those of the United Nations. In many cases the method of nominating is spelled out; in some,
submission of biographical details is mandatory. Many agencies have time frames, rules for the
submission of candidatures, and procedures in case no candidate receives the requisite majority.
The adoption by WHO, in 1996, of criteria for selection of its Director-General is notable.

The terms of office of the executive heads vary from three to six years, and in all cases heads
may be reappointed at least once. Some, however, have remained in office for very long periods;
the record is twenty-five years, but four others served more than twenty and a recent FAO head
served eighteen years.

---

[11]   *Who Speaks for the Hungry: How FAO elects its leader* (Uppsala, Dag Hammarskjöld Foundation, 1996).
[12]   Discussed in detail in the authors' *Renewing the United Nations System* (Uppsala, Dag Hammarskjöld Foundation,
       Development Dialogue 1994:1), page 66 et seq.

▶ **Table 1.   Nationalities of UN system executive heads,
1946–1996**

Nationality	Number of executive heads [1]	Per cent	Nationality	Number of executive heads [1]	Per cent
USA	39	25.0	Philippines	2	1.3
Switzerland	11	7.0	Tunisia	2	1.3
France	9	6.0	Turkey	2	1.3
UK	9	6.0	Algeria	1	.64
Canada	8	5.0	Austria	1	.64
Sweden	7	4.5	Burma	1	.64
Brazil	5	3.0	Cameroon	1	.64
India	5	3.0	El Salvador	1	.64
Netherlands	5	3.0	Finland	1	.64
Denmark	4	3.0	Gambia	1	.64
Egypt	4	3.0	Ghana	1	.64
Italy	4	3.0	Indonesia	1	.64
Senegal	3	2.0	Iran	1	.64
Argentina	2	1.3	Kuwait	1	.64
Australia	2	1.3	Pakistan	1	.64
Belgium	2	1.3	Peru	1	.64
Ireland	2	1.3	Saudi Arabia	1	.64
Japan	2	1.3	Sierra Leone	1	.64
Lebanon	2	1.3	Spain	1	.64
Mexico	2	1.3	Sri Lanka	1	.64
Nigeria	2	1.3	Venezuela	1	.64
Norway	2	1.3			
Totals				155	101.1

[1]   For this and other tables a person serving multiple terms in an executive position was counted once. The same person serving as executive head of two separate UN organizations at different times was counted twice. Total percentages slightly exceed 100.0 due to rounding-off.

There have been some brilliant appointments; other promising candidates have, once in office, belied the hopes vested in them; and governments have made some disastrous choices.

In some Specialized Agencies the head is almost always from within the organization; in most from outside it; in some, invariably of Western nationality. Table 1 assembles the fifty-year pattern of nationalities of UN system executive heads.[13]

▶ *Nationalities*

The aggregate pattern revealed in Table 1 has inevitable political implications. For example, the table thoroughly refutes the widespread canard that 'the UN system is dominated by the Third World majority'. The statistical analysis discloses the following key facts:

---

[13]   For all purposes in this study 'executive heads of the UN system' means officials elected or appointed to head distinct organizations, funds, or programmes at USG or higher rank.

Brian
Urquhart

Erskine
Childers

A   WORLD   IN   NEED
OF   LEADERSHIP :
TOMORROW'S   UNITED   NATIONS
– A   FRESH   APPRAISAL –

▶ Citizens from about one fifth of the **185 UN** member countries have so far filled the **155** incumbencies in **UN**-system executive-head posts since **1946**.

▶ Nationals of the United States have held **25** per cent of all executive-head positions in the system.

▶ Taking the three Western permanent members of the **UN** Security Council together their nationals have, over the half-century, held **37** per cent of all incumbencies (no national of either China or Russia has held an executive post in the system to date).

▶ Overall, nationals of Western countries have filled **109** incumbencies, or **70** per cent of the total in the system since **1946**.

Contrary to a widespread assumption, a Western predominance was not inevitable in the period before decolonization; even in 1945 at the founding of the UN, 33 of the 51 members were countries of Latin America and the Caribbean (20), Asia (5), the Arab world (5) and Africa (3). Given so heavy a Western predominance in the leadership over the fifty years as a whole, it is important to see how much of it occurred before, and how much has persisted since, decolonization.

Table 2 analyses whether the advent of the Third World's majority after decolonization— thereafter some 75 per cent of the membership—significantly affected this overall Western hold on the system's leadership.

▶ *Table 2.   Regional sources of leaders, pre- and post-decolonization and as of 1996* [1]

Region of origin	Number of appointments & per cent of total							
	1946–70	%	1970–96	%	1946–96	%	In 1996 [5]	%
Western Europe [2]	33	46	29	35	62	40	9	34.6
Eastern Europe	0		0		0		0	
North America	24	33	23	28	47	30	7	27.0
Latin America	6	8	6	7	12	8	3	11.5
Caribbean	0		0		0			
Arab States	2	3	9	11	11	7	2	7.7
Africa (sub-Sahara)	2	3	7	8	9	6	3	11.5
Asia-Pacific	5	7	9	11	14	9	2	7.7
Totals	72 [3]	100	83 [4]	100	155	100	26	100

[1] The majority of former colonies achieved independence by 1962. However, to allow for such factors as completion of existing incumbencies, the advent of some important new organizations and the reorganization of others, 1970 was chosen as the base year from which to analyse possible regional shifts in executive leadership in the system resulting from decolonization.

[2] Includes Australia.

[3] Includes appointments that in some cases extended beyond 1970.

[4] The practice of multiple terms of office, and recent restructuring slightly reducing the number of USG heads, affects the total number of new appointments.

[5] Figures for all incumbencies in the single year 1996.

After decolonization there was a decrease between 1970 and 1990 in the percentage of posts held by Western European and North American nationals, from the earlier 79 per cent of all incumbencies 1946-1970, as shown in Table 2, to 62 per cent from 1946-1990 (not shown). This has not significantly changed in more recent years: as of 1996 Western nationals still held virtually 62 per cent of all executive-head posts in the system. This, however, represented a continued tenure of the majority of posts by nationals of a 25 per cent minority of member states.

The above analysis covers the incumbencies in all executive-head posts in the UN system, in large and smaller organizations.

Global political factors have played major roles in the larger among these organizations. Table 3 analyses the regional sources of incumbencies in 17 larger organizations of the system over the fifty years.

Although these are the larger organizations in the system, the different characteristics among them make overall conclusions from the statistics of more limited value. The 17 organizations include the UN and five Specialized Agencies in which voting is by majorities of universal membership; three weighted-voting financial agencies (IBRD, IMF and IFAD); and six

▶ **Table 3.   Regional sources of leadership of major organizations, 1946–1996**

UN Body	Western Europe	North America	Latin America	Arab States	Asia	Africa sub-Sahara
UN	3		1	1[1]	1	
UNICEF		3				
UNCTAD			3		1	1
UNDP	1	5				
UNEP	1	2		1		
UNFPA					2	
UNRWA	4	6				
UNHCR	6				2	
WFP	2[2]	3	2			
ILO	4	1				
FAO	2	2		1	1	1
UNESCO	5	2	1			1
WHO	1	1	1		1	
IFAD				3		
UNIDO			1		1	
IBRD		9				
IMF	7					
Totals	36 (37%)	34 (35%)	9 (9%)	6 (6%)	9 (10%)	3 (3%)

[1]   Mr. Boutros-Ghali was elected as an African candidate: he is shown in this table as a national of an Arab State for uniformity of analysis by nationality.
[2]   Includes the then Australian incumbent, James C. Ingram.

Brian
Urquhart

Erskine
Childers

A WORLD IN NEED
OF LEADERSHIP:
TOMORROW'S UNITED NATIONS
- A FRESH APPRAISAL -

UN voluntarily financed funds and programmes in most of which 'donor' country influences on leadership choices are strong.

With this qualification, however, the overall results are not significantly different from those derived from the full composition of the UN system in Table 2. Once again there is no sign of the legendary 'Third World domination'. Among 98 incumbencies, monopolies abound.

▸ **All ILO's Directors-General have come from either Western Europe (4) or North America (1), with no change since decolonization. All IMF Managing Directors (7) have been Western European. All the World Bank's Presidents (9) have been United States nationals. All UNDP's Administrators have been American (5) except for David Owen (United Kingdom), briefly a UNDP co-Administrator. All UNICEF's Executive Directors (4) have been Americans. All UNRWA's directors have been either North American (6) or West European (4). An almost unbroken West European monopoly on the leadership of UNHCR (6 of 7 posts until 1993) is currently broken by a Japanese incumbent, Ms Ogata.**
▸ **The only monopolies outside of the North are that the heads of IFAD have been Arab and UNCTAD has had a spread of Southern nationalities. UNFPA has only been headed by citizens of developing countries although not by any 'tradition'.**
▸ **Of the other major and long-established Specialized Agencies, 5 out of 7 UNESCO Directors-General have been Western. Only in FAO and WHO has there been a significant spread of regional sources of their heads.**
▸ **Overall, since 1946 nationals of Western Europe and North America have held 72 per cent of all the posts in these major organizations of the system. By 1996, however, the effect of decolonization is showing in a considerably lower proportion, 53 per cent, of these 17 posts held by nationals of Western Europe (4) and North America (5). However, counting by proportions of the membership or world population this is still more than twice those regions' combined strength.**

There has also been a considerable concentration of nationalities within regions. Of Europe's 62 appointments since 1946, 45 have been nationals of only 6 European countries.[14] Of Latin America's 12 incumbencies 9 have come from Brazil, Argentina and Mexico. A spreading of appointments is, however, evident in the last twenty years and this is likely to continue.

In more ideal circumstances all executive-head posts in the system would be filled by 'only the best', found from serious searching and regardless of nationality or region. The long background of Western predominance makes moving towards such a goal more difficult, and attempts to change or defensive action to preserve the present overall leadership pattern more likely.

A listing of all the men (and the very few women) who have held executive-head posts in

---

[14] The number of Swiss incumbencies in part reflects Switzerland's historical roles in refugee matters and hosting of (UNHCR), and equivalent special roles in the Universal Postal Union (UPU).

each organization of the UN system since its establishment may be found at the end of this study in Table 8. Taken all in all it is an impressive list that includes many significant leaders of the international community in the last half-century. For choosing those leaders governments deserve praise; but their right choices only indicate that they *can* choose well. They have by no means always done so.

Moreover, the optimum contribution of even the best executive heads has never been possible because, to date in the UN system, these distinguished public servants have not been able to work as a commanding team on the world's economic and social problems. Before going into details of the selection process it is important to examine this overall problem.

▶ The team that never was

> Times go by turns, and chances change by course,
> From foul to fair, from better hap to worse ...
>
> *Robert Southwell* [15]

Table 4 sets out a calendar of all the recent and all the projected executive-head appointments and elections in the UN system between 1994 and 2003. *Such a calendar is not published anywhere in the official United Nations system.* This in itself reflects a fundamental weakness—the impossibility, in the system as it presently operates, of a collective leadership that could be more than a group of separately executive offices.

The chronology of appointments is such that in a Secretary-General's first year of office member-states appoint only 2 of the major specialized agency executive heads. The new appointments of the other major agency heads occur before and later in the Secretary-General's term.

The generally scattered chronology of appointment is not deliberate. The sectoral officials within each government who decide in each agency on its electoral calendar seldom meet even their own national counterparts in the other agencies to discuss these, or indeed any other, common questions in the UN system. The timings are largely derived from the year of first appointment in each individual organization decades ago.

Member-governments thus deny themselves and the international community any possibility of a UN-system team integrally planned for any future period. Nor can any Secretary-General exert significant influence over the composition of the team he or she is supposed to lead. [16]

---

[15] A poem written in 1595. 'Hap' was a contemporary word for 'by chance'.

[16] Questions concerning the selection and appointment of the heads of such funds as UNDP, UNFPA, UNICEF etc. are treated separately later in this chapter. In the past even these appointments have lacked proper attention by Secretaries-General. The heads of the funds are not formally members of the Administrative Committee on Co-ordination (ACC), but for many years until the advent of Secretary-General Boutros-Ghali were allowed to sit in it on an apparently co-equal basis with the heads of the Specialized Agencies despite some vehement objections. Mr. Boutros-Ghali has insisted that he, as Secretary-General speaks for them in that body.

Brian
Urquhart

Erskine
Childers

A   WORLD   IN   NEED
OF   LEADERSHIP:
TOMORROW'S   UNITED   NATIONS
- A   FRESH   APPRAISAL -

▶ **Table 4.   Leadership elections/appointments from 1994 to 2003**[1]

Head	1994	1995	1996	1997	1998	1999	2000	2001	2002	2003
UN S-G			●					●		
UNCHS		●				●				
UNCTAD		●				●				●
UNDCP [2]										
UNDP				●				●		
UNEP			●				●			
UNFPA		●				●				●
UNHCR					●					●
UNICEF		●					●			
UNRWA			●			●			●	
UNU				●					●	
WFP				●					●	
IAEA				●				●		
ILO	●					●				
FAO						●				
UNESCO						●				
WHO					●					●
IBRD			●				●			
IMF				●					●	
ICAO	●			●			●			●
UPU	●					●				
ITU	●				●				●	
WMO			●			●				●
IMO				●				●		
WIPO				●						●
IFAD				●				●		
UNIDO				●				●		
(WTO) [3]		●				●				
Totals [4]	4	7	3	10	3	10	4	6	5	7

[1] This table has been adjusted from the original in the First Edition to reflect closures and other changes in the organizations or terms of office of the system. It shows elections and appointments for ten years from 1994 in order to illustrate their spread in relation to the appointment years (1996 and 2001) of the UN Secretary-General on present term of office.

[2] Appointment years undetermined.

[3] The World Trade Organization is included because according to UN Charter Article 57 it should be brought into relationship with the UN and the system as a Specialized Agency. At time of preparation of this edition this has not yet been done.

[4] Totals include both elections to Agency posts and appointments to UN funds by the UN Secretary-General, and therefore combine different processes. The value of the totals is only that they show how scattered are all the starting-points of all executive-head relative to the start of an S-G term of office.

Yet as has already been stressed, increasingly the system is challenged by world needs that do not divide themselves neatly into the traditional sectors, but require comprehensive forward strategies and sound inter-agency action. In a nation state a good Prime Minister will realise that, for example, Agriculture will need a particular development for a number of years, and that the country's trade initiatives will have to reinforce this. A good Secretary-General should be able to perceive the global equivalent of such special inter-sectoral needs over his or her term of office, and seek an appropriate UN-system team to respond to them.

At present, however, a Secretary-General cannot even attempt such efforts, given the calendar. This is not because some earlier policy of governments was reversed; there never has been any policy to build the system's leadership around the Secretary-General of the United Nations and the world's pressing future needs.

Governments should adopt a comprehensive new policy-approach to executive leadership in the United Nations system, which should include a decision to re-phase the timing of appointments of heads in alignment with that of the Secretary-General.

▶ Governance of the system as system

One of the reasons for the lack of any common policy-approach to leadership is that the UN system as such has no inter-governmental body to bind its component organizations together and to direct it *as* a system. The UN Economic and Social Council (ECOSOC) is mandated to co-ordinate the activities of the Specialized Agencies, but among many reasons why this has not to date been successful is that the sectors of member governments that participate in the Agencies are not the same as those in ECOSOC.

The authors of this study have made detailed recommendations on these problems elsewhere.[17] Here, a key recommendation should be noted, that the General Assembly should establish a United Nations System Consultative Board comprising the members of the Bureau of ECOSOC; the Bureaux of the executive governing bodies of the major agencies; and one representative of each other agency. This would provide the essential, and to date missing, instrument in which member governments could formulate common policy-approaches on all matters that need the combined effort of the system.

▶ Intergovernmental selection machinery

At some level in each separate mechanism of each organization of the system, its member governments jointly elect or confirm the appointment of its executive head. Here again there is no common approach.

In some organizations governments use a smaller, though representative, executive body (Council or Board) to approve nominations; in others, the nominations come directly from individual governments to the full electing body.

The differences have not arisen from particularities in the work of a given agency. They

---

[17] In *Renewing the United Nations System, op. cit., passim*, but in the immediate context especially pages 62 and 190-191.

Brian
Urquhart

Erskine
Childers

*A   WORLD   IN   NEED
OF   LEADERSHIP:
TOMORROW'S   UNITED   NATIONS
- A   FRESH   APPRAISAL -*

were decided decades ago, by delegations coming from different departments of the
governments of the same member states. The people concerned with each agency have grown up
with their particular structure, which has acquired a life and rationale of its own. As will be
noted, in the relatively few instances where the rules about executive heads have been debated,
the absence of any common policy for the UN system has usually favoured the status quo.

Table 5 sets out the basic facts.

▶ Table 5. Elected executive head posts: selection procedure[1]

Organ	Term of office		Procedures for election				
	Years	No. of terms [2]	Time-table [3]	Nomina-tion [4]	Search [5]	Scrutiny [6]	Approve
UN	5	No limit	No	State/SC	No	None	UN GA
ILO	5	No limit	Yes	State	No	None	Gov. Body
FAO	6	No limit	Yes	State	No	None	FAO Conf.
UNESCO	6	Two	Yes	State/EB	No	Yes	Gen. Conf.
WHO	5	No limit	Yes	State/EB	No	Yes	Assembly
ICAO	3	No limit	Yes	State	No	Yes	Council
UPU	5	Two	No	State	No	None	Congress
ITU	4	Two	No	State	No	None	Plen. Conf
WMO	4	No limit	No	State	No	None	Congress
IMO	4	No limit	Yes	Council	No	Yes	Counc./Ass
WIPO	6	No limit	No	Coord.Comm.	No	Yes	WIPO GA
IFAD	4	Two	No	State	No	No	Gov. Counc.
UNIDO	4	Two	Yes	Dev. Bd.	No	Yes	Gen. Conf.
IAEA	4	No limit	No	Bd. Govs.	No	Yes	Gen. Conf.
IBRD	5	No limit	Yes	Ex. Bd.	No	Yes	Exec. Bd.
IMF	5	No limit	Yes	Ex. Bd.	No	Yes	Exec. Bd.
UNU	5	Two	Yes	UN/UNESCO	Yes	Yes	Council

[1] This table deals only with the intergovernmentally filled posts of UN S-G and of heads of the Specialized Agencies.
Procedures for heads of UN funds/programmes appointed by the Secretary-General with only confirmation by an
intergovernmental body are analysed in Table 7.

[2] Whether the incumbency is renewable and if so for how many further terms. 'Two' signifies a maximum of one
additional term.

[3] Whether there is an official, prescribed timetable for procedures, i.e. date by which nominations must be received,
are closed, et cetera.

[4] 'State' and another body means that a Member State nominates but an intergovernmental body forwards the
nomination to the electoral body.

[5] Whether there is an official, organized search for candidates beyond those promoting their own nomination.

[6] Whether nominees are formally examined for their qualities and qualifications.

▶ *A vicious circle*

It will be evident from the foregoing that the overall problems of leadership selection have long roots. These problems have been exacerbated by the widening North-South political and economic divide, and by the effort by a minority of member states, and especially by major powers among them, to retain the prerogatives of a majority.

The system has not developed the capacity it was originally supposed to have to tackle global socio-economic problems coherently. Notwithstanding pockets of improved income among and within some developing countries, the North-South 'poverty gap' has relentlessly widened. In turn, under a widespread and erroneous belief that this is due to failures or weaknesses in the administration of *development assistance*, Northern 'donor' governments have intensified the concept of conditionality. All member governments contribute to such development cooperation according to their relative capacities; all are in fact 'donors'. Again, however, applying a concept that is alien to the principles of the UN Charter, 'donor' countries have claimed that since they contribute the most (in financial amounts), they must have a predominating influence over the economic and social components of the UN system, maintaining what is now a minority predominance in executive leadership, with diminished or indifferent support to the organizations in the system that are led by nationals of developing countries. The system's capacity for effective leadership on vital world economic and social needs has been kept weak, and it has not been able to take major steps to moderate the widening North-South gap.

Specific aspects of selection and appointment need to be examined with the foregoing problems and factors in mind. It is a basic contention of this study that the system's executive heads should be *found* by a deliberate search for the best at any given time. To assess the validity of this position it is first necessary to see how the heads are presently selected.

III. SCREENING

Gouverner, c'est choisir.
The Duc de Lévis [18]

Even without a deliberate external search for best candidates, screening of those who are nominated should be an obvious minimal measure by governments. Screening is more than merely eliminating candidates by conversations and cables and 'straw polls' and ending up with the least controversial one. At the least it should mean a serious examination of qualities and qualifications. As Table 5 shows, however, even this minimum requirement is not standard throughout the system.

▶ Screening in the UN-proper

In the Security Council process for nomination for Secretary-General there is to date no organised screening of candidates of any kind. It has been suggested that the 'veto filter' is a kind of screening, but it is not exercised by the Council as a body, and is for the most part based only on the narrow interests or biasses of a given Permanent Member. Genuine screening would obviously provide that all nominees could be viewed by the whole membership of the responsible body on equal terms, without any candidate starting with a special disadvantage. The continued retention of veto power in the selection of the Secretary-General is therefore a major obstacle to proper screening.

Astonishingly, however, among all the other United Nations appointment processes for executive heads of funds and programmes where the permanent members have no veto power, there are only two instances of any kind of screening of candidates. UNRWA's Advisory Commission, and the Council of UNU, have screening roles. As will be seen in a later section dealing with the heads of the UN development and humanitarian funds (UNDP etc.), there is no screening of candidates for these highly responsible posts.

▶ Screening in the Agencies

As Table 5 shows, screening in the Specialized Agencies is more evident but by no means universal. In most cases where a body does formally examine candidacies it does so perfunctorily, and on paper only.

At perhaps the other extreme in the UN-system pattern, any member state can nominate a candidate to be Director-General of FAO, and that nomination goes straight to FAO's full-membership Conference where balloting must immediately take place. FAO's

---

[18] 'To govern is to choose.' In *Maximes et Reflexions*, 1812.

executive body, the Council, is not involved. Charles Weitz observes that, 'In any method in which the Council had a role there would be ample time and room for the total membership of FAO to balance all essential inputs, political and other, before the final decision'.

▶ *The range of screening*

Merely having a smaller representative intergovernmental body conduct a screening as such does not, of course, guarantee the best selection of candidates. The screening functions of such a body can range all the way from only verifying basic data in a *curriculum vitae*; through examining the qualifications of candidates as nominations are received; on to the body constituting itself a Search Committee actually to *look* for the best candidates, and then screening those on a short list in person.

▶ *Transparency*

Of course, the smaller the body responsible for preparing nominations, the less transparent the process may be. In the parts of the system where such mechanisms are already used they have not infrequently resulted in reports of 'secret deals' and 'donor-plays', for posts that should command wide international public confidence (and should never be filled by a national merely because of a government's level of financial contribution to the organization).

In respect of the Secretary-Generalship this study has already urged that not only governments but parliamentarians, NGOs, and individual citizens should have the opportunity to recommend candidates, and at the mid-stage to comment on a short list derived from a positive search. No such procedure exists at present anywhere in the UN system. Striking the right balance between wide participation and a necessary minimum of confidentiality at key stages in the process is crucial to real improvement.

▶ *Change in WHO*

An example of major improvement in the use of a Board, following much recent controversy, may be seen in the World Health Organization's amendment of its Constitution in 1996.[19] That organization has now adopted *criteria* which a candidate for the post of Director-General must henceforth fulfil.

---

[19] Resolution EB97.R10 of the Executive Board of WHO adopted on 23 January 1996.

Brian
Urquhart

Erskine
Childers

A   WORLD   IN   NEED
OF   LEADERSHIP :
TOMORROW 'S   UNITED   NATIONS
- A   FRESH   APPRAISAL -

WHO's new criteria for Director-General:

- ▸ a strong technical and public health background and extensive experience in international health;
- ▸ competency in organizational management;
- ▸ proven historical evidence for public health leadership;
- ▸ sensitiveness to cultural, social and political differences;
- ▸ a strong commitment to the work of **WHO**;
- ▸ the good physical condition required of all staff members of the Organization; and
- ▸ sufficient skill in at least one of the official and working languages of the Executive Board and World Health Assembly.

In addition to this significant new prescription of criteria, nominations for Director-General of WHO may henceforth be submitted by any member state, not only by members of the Board. A deadline before the next Board meeting of two months rather than two weeks is now stipulated for receipt of nominations. Of great importance, the nominations must henceforth be sent (with supporting information in the appropriate language) to Board members one month before the meeting, where formerly they got them only at the meeting on its opening day.

More significantly again, the WHO Board will conduct an 'initial screening' of all candidates 'in order to eliminate those candidates not meeting the criteria'. The Board will then assemble a short list from the remaining candidates. Two weeks later in its session these selected candidates will be *interviewed* by the whole Board, each making a presentation and answering questions. After this substantive screening the Board will elect one of the candidates on the short list by secret ballot.

The new procedure, however, remains passive; the amending resolution does not prescribe any kind of active external search.

IV.   WHAT IS A NOMINATION?

You will find it a very good practice always to verify your references, Sir !
Martin J. Routh [20]

An important question is how someone should come to be nominated in the first place. Governments of member states formalize nominations, but what should be meant by 'government'?

A person can obtain a letter from a given government official 'nominating' him or her to one of these high posts without the central machinery of the same government being aware of it. Charles Weitz notes that in the 1993 FAO election for Director-General, 'several candidates did not have the full support of their governments ... only later, as the campaign began to unfold, did other parts of the government become aware of the implications of what had been done in the name of "the government" '.

Such episodes are an indication of the degree of importance which top national officials attach to the United Nations and its system, and the extent of effort to achieve greater cohesion among a member-state's various departments that participate in the system's different branches.[21] And here again there is need for a common policy by governments throughout the system. Such a policy should ensure the genuine support of the *Government* for a candidate, and have the useful additional feature of ensuring its serious attention to the election.

All nominations to executive-head posts in the system should be expected to come from the Office of an executive President or Prime Minister.[22]

▶ Multi-government endorsement?

So far we have only dealt with the nomination of a national by his or her own government. Charles Weitz suggests that 'a nominating government could be expected to convince at least ten or twelve like-minded governments that its candidate was worthy of written support', and that it should, therefore, present, with its nomination, letters of support from a prescribed minimum number of other governments. This prescription might usefully cover support from each region of the world.

---

[20] The English classicist, in J.W. Burgon, *Lives of Twelve Good Men*, Vol. 1, p. 73, 1888.
[21] As a most recent example of the efforts by some governments to achieve such coherence, in its 1996 White Paper on Foreign Policy the Irish Government announced the establishment of an 'Inter-Departmental Liaison Group to ensure a more focused national position in the various UN bodies'; White Paper of 26 March 1996, Dublin.
[22] In many instances in such a procedure the chief-executive office would receive the relevant letter for signature from the Foreign Office. We recommend that the signatory and issuing office be that of the chief executive because one of the abiding tensions within governments concerning the UN system is between the Foreign Office and sectoral ministries which handle policy in the specialized agencies.

V.   TERMS OF OFFICE

I have more care to stay than will to go ...

Shakespeare [23]

The issue of renewability of the terms of office for executive posts runs like a thread through all other aspects of the leadership question. Its pervasive influence is both obvious and largely ignored. Closely intertwined with *length* of term, the issue of renewability deserves detailed discussion, beginning with posing the basic arguments.

▶ The case for renewability

The arguments in favour of the renewability of an incumbent's term in a UN leadership post can be stated quite briefly. If an outstanding person is in the post and has perhaps even grown in the position, why deprive the organization and the international community of such leadership and experience?

The second argument in favour of renewability is that of continuity and steadiness. Why rock the boat if it is on a reasonably sound course? This argument may attain greater weight if the incumbent is still engaged in some major improvement or innovation as the first term draws to a close, or if some major international crisis is impending or still in process.

Here the issue of *length* of term becomes important. Understandably, if a leadership term is of only four or five years, and the incumbent is doing well enough or is carrying out important initiatives, the argument for renewal may seem overwhelming. The main issue, however, is the length of the term. If it were somewhat longer, a single term of office would be sufficient for any important innovation.

A third, much more circumspect, argument for renewability is that it sometimes protects an organization from the election of some 'undesirable' candidate who may have overwhelming political influence behind him or her. This argument has arisen not so much in general debate about terms of office but in regard to a few posts over which a member state has held a 'traditional' monopoly. A sharp domestic political change in such a state might open a post about to be vacated to a candidate without qualifications for running the organization concerned or, indeed, the necessary respect for UN precepts and principles. In such a case, renewability allows the retention of a known quantity; a poor enough reason since it derives from national monopoly, but one that has on occasion been used.

▶ The case against renewability

Whether or not one accepts the first part of Lord Acton's often-quoted dictum, that 'all power corrupts', the knowledge that one could be re-elected or reappointed can be, and on occasion has

---

[23]   Juliet in William Shakespeare's *Romeo and Juliet*, III.5.1, 1595.

been, a dangerous psychological influence in the mind (and in the inner office) of an executive head. Even some who have previously shown no trace whatever of excessive self-esteem or vaulting ambition have proved vulnerable to these insidious influences:

- The first time an important Ambassador or other national official arrives, and includes in the discussion a mild suggestion about recruiting a favoured citizen into the Secretariat, the danger may manifest itself. [24] The national's biography may reveal no reason why he/she should *not* be recruited into UN service; the question whether it contains decisive evidence that he *should* is the one that may not be asked.
- Policy issues may arise where the executive head's views will be important. Will he court the certain displeasure of some delegations if a small voice is reminding him that they are his constituents in a future election?
- Situations may call for an important public initiative by the executive head which one or more governments may not welcome. Will he or she go forward with it?
- Almost invariably, an executive head has staff some of whom increasingly perceive their own careers as invested in his, and may tell him that he is 'indispensable'. Such staff hinder, or even halt all consideration of a replacement by the mere intimation to delegates that the incumbent is 'thinking of standing again'.
- The media and public will tend to judge every action and statement of the Secretary-General as a move to be re-elected, regardless of the Secretary-General's actual motives or intentions.

Charles Weitz has traced the long history of the debates among Delegations to FAO Conferences about the renewability or not of its Directors-General. Several valuable points emerge from this, the only comprehensive intergovernmental debate on these issues in the UN system.

- The issue first arose, not over the merits or demerits of renewability as such, but over the personality of a distinguished and determined (some felt, too determined) incumbent in the post, B.R. Sen of India.
- In the first round of this debate the outcome was a decision for a 4-year term renewable for up to two further 2-year terms (the '4+2+2 formula', as it became known).
- In later years many delegates argued that any such formula would deflect an incumbent from real work into almost continuous electioneering, and that four years was too short to make a distinctive contribution.
- In 1971 the FAO Conference adopted a single non-renewable term of six years, under which rule Edouard Saouma (Lebanon) was elected Director-General in 1975. He promptly moved to restore renewability—unlimited—and served three terms, for a total of 18 years.

---

[24] Soon after he first assumed the office, Secretary-General Pérez de Cuellar made a point of publicly declaring that he would only serve one term, adding that it was important that all concerned know this so that he might be free of pressure. In the event, he stood again and served a second term. Soon after assuming office Secretary-General Boutros-Ghali announced that he intended to serve only one term; in 1995 he told media that 'only someone stupid never changes his mind'.

Brian
Urquhart

Erskine
Childers

A   W O R L D   I N   N E E D
O F   L E A D E R S H I P :
T O M O R R O W ' S   U N I T E D   N A T I O N S
- A   F R E S H   A P P R A I S A L -

When the FAO Council later discussed the reversal back to unlimited terms, one of the arguments used to support it was that renewability prevailed elsewhere in the UN system. In UNESCO, at the 1989 General Conference, the Constitution was amended, limiting an incumbent to two six-year terms. Here again, the practice in the rest of the UN system was raised in the debate, the Chairman of the Legal Committee recalling that various delegations had spoken of the desirability of a similar step in other organizations.

It seems clear that a General Assembly decision for a single term of seven years for United Nations Secretaries-General—as the present study urges—would be essential to provide the leadership in the system necessary to end unlimited terms of office for all executive heads.

▶ Abuses in elections

To the list of arguments in favour of a single term may be added the dangers of deliberate actions by an incumbent to ensure re-election, using the powers and resources of office. These have occurred from time to time throughout the history of UN system leadership. Such behaviour has included manipulation of recruitment and other personnel procedures; the steering of project funds towards important sources of votes; the intimidation of permanent representatives near election time by high-level manoeuvres directly with their home governments; the intimidation of international civil servants into active campaigning for the incumbent's re-election; actions taken to obtain awards or secure personal publicity; and the use of the executive head's valuable time and travel funds for journeys seeking re-election votes.

A serious problem arises over such stories, whose repeated media ventilation damages the credibility of the whole UN system: *governments have very seldom initiated any official enquiry about them.* By far the largest volume of such stories has come from FAO yet, as Charles Weitz notes in his study, 'at no time during the period when these allegations were most frequent have member governments, acting either through the FAO Council or the General Conference, tabled the questions or held any formal enquiry'.

Governments themselves have not been free of abusive practices in the history of elections. There have been instances of a government supporting a candidate in return for promises of a high-level post being 'assigned' to that power; many more instances of wealthy governments pressing on weak ones to direct their votes to a candidate, or threatening to reduce their contributions to a UN fund if their national is challenged by another.

Clearly, the scope for abuse will be drastically reduced by the single action of instituting non-renewable terms of office throughout the system. But when governments fail to carry out proper, independent enquiries about any serious allegations of abuse they are as directly responsible for the damage done to the credibility of the UN system as any culpable individual may be.

Governments have in recent years been compelled in many parts of the world to institute official, legal enquiries into fraud and other malpractice in national elections, including those in many democracies. Citizens should hold their governments to no less account under the international law of the Charter and the system's other constitutions for the equivalent obligation to protect the integrity of elections of its executive heads. Legal prohibitions should be incorporated in the General Assembly resolution which this study recommends. The following would still be essential even with single terms of office system-wide.

Needed legal prohibitions

▶ The pledging to any government of any post, or any other special privilege by a candidate is illegal. If found to have been committed by an unsuccessful candidate he or she shall be disbarred from all further candidatures or other employment in the **UN** system; if by a successful candidate he or she shall be removed from office;

▶ The pledging *by* any government of additional financial contributions or any other material benefit to the organization if a national is elected is illegal.

▶ The practice by any member state of any form of economic coercion or suborning to obtain the votes of another member state for any candidate shall result in the election being declared void.

▶ *The danger of error*

> An election is coming. Universal Peace is declared. And the foxes have a
> sincere interest in prolonging the lives of the poultry ...
> *George Eliot (Mary Ann Evans)* [25]

It is axiomatic that there is no perfect, error-proof process for selecting public leaders. Someone who has shown great promise may fail to rise to the actual challenge of a post. Someone who has served well as the head of another kind of organization can turn out to be a relative mediocrity in a major UN agency. Someone whose autocratic ways were tolerable in some smaller agency outside the UN can be revealed in a large UN body as an arrogant unguided missile. Or the unassuming, quiet personage of yesterday can become an incipient megalomaniac in high office in a UN organization. Some of the more disastrous appointments made by governments to these posts in the past can clearly be attributed to indifference, to the politics of the lowest common denominator, or to East-West or North-South tensions or differences; but some have been straightforward errors in judgment. Improvements in rules and procedures will not fully guarantee against errors, but would certainly provide some greater protection against them.

It is, however, also vital that the UN system's leadership be *capable of change when change is clearly needed.* In addition, amid changes in world needs—and perhaps a major restructuring

---

[25] In *Felix Holt*, ch. 5, 1866.

Brian
Urquhart

Erskine
Childers

A   WORLD   IN   NEED
OF   LEADERSHIP:
TOMORROW'S   UNITED   NATIONS
- A   FRESH   APPRAISAL -

of an organization—a leader who has been good for one period may not necessarily be the most appropriate for the one ahead. The tradition of renewability of an incumbent is a serious obstacle to the system's capacity for well-considered change and development.

▶ The incumbent's advantages

In national public leadership, an incumbent has very powerful built-in advantages over any contestant; but in the UN system an incumbent is in some respects even more favoured. The following description could apply to virtually all intergovernmental organizations (IGOs):

> A main, perhaps the main, basis for leadership by an executive head of an IGO is the respect accorded the position as the primary institutional representation of the organization. In even the least complex IGO, there is multiplicity—of members, of organs, of tasks, of programmes. The more complex is the organization, the more multiplex are its components and its emanations and the more difficult it is for the organization to identify itself, to be identified, amid the multiple claims to define its ethos. Only one actor is available to fill this identity vacuum and that is the executive head. Constitutionally neutral, the executive head is in a position to attract the confidences of all and, thus, is enabled to claim their confidence as well.[26]

The aura that can build up around this personage can soften—and has softened—criticism of an incumbent at crucial junctures.

Other powerful factors can work to the advantage of the incumbent who is eligible for another term. There is nothing like as much patronage to dispense to loyal supporters as in national politics; but an incumbent in the UN system usually has behind him his government and his region *vis-à-vis* other regions, either or both of which other governments may not wish to offend by supporting a new candidate.

▶ The North-South factor

The strong economic, political and cultural tensions across the North-South divide have sometimes made re-electing an incumbent from a developing country an issue not only of his competence and behaviour in office, but also of resisting Western pressures or donor-country conditions. An incumbent may be able to mobilize Third World majority support for himself.[27] He may also greatly strengthen his position if he is able to point to Northern opposition to a Third World incumbent concurrently heading another UN agency. Developing countries may well have misgivings about renewing an incompetent or mediocre executive head; but while the

---

[26] Lawrence S. Finkelstein, in ed. Finkelstein, *Politics in the United Nations System* (Durham, Duke University Press, 1988), p. 409.

[27] Needless to say, when Western majorities prevailed the same syndromes noted here could be observed.

renewability of terms continues, and as long as North-South tensions persist or increase, factors of solidarity and resistance to a potential insult to the Third World as a whole may be important in the selection process.[28]

The obvious solution to such problems is the single term of office. If left free to vote their own choices the developing countries' majority in many agencies provides the possibility of electing or approving a new and better person, even from their regions. A single term would remove from the selection process any suggestion of bowing to Northern pressure or acquiescing in derogation of a Third World head in another agency.

A single term would also protect the organization and the system from the longer-term harm that can be done if a major power uses its special influence to secure the appointment of an inadequate or damaging person who then gains re-appointment.

▶ Other political factors

North-South tension is not the only cause of the renewal of an executive head whose performance has been less than brilliant. There can be situations near the end of a term of office where the incumbent is from a country whose government various other members do not wish to displease at that particular time. Key ministers of such governments have decided that they should 'reserve their credit' with that particular government for more important controversies which may have absolutely nothing to do with the UN organization concerned, but which override the policy considerations on the UN issue. On more than one occasion this disregard of vital UN-system needs has occurred among Northern governments.

The situation in the UN's own funds and programmes will be discussed separately later in this chapter. Here, however, it is important to note that renewability of terms can have especially severe consequences where there is no formal involvement of a governing body, as is the case in the selection procedures for virtually all executive heads of the funds and programmes. The Secretary-General is supposed only to 'consult' the members of the governing body separately and privately. There being no *voting* procedure either in the immediate governing body or in the General Assembly which merely and nominally 'confirms', the Secretary-General has sometimes been at the mercy of a form of unspoken consensus. He has not wished to take the risk of proposing a replacement of the incumbent, even if he has known this *should* be done and that many governments wished it *could* be done, lest delegations anxious not to offend the incumbent's government fail to support his action. As long as member governments permit their non-UN diplomatic relationships to affect their positions over vital posts, the Secretary-General

---

[28] It may be noted here that the role of Third World majorities in the election of Third World candidates has been exaggerated by Northern media. Edouard Saouma was widely described as such a candidate but, as Charles Weitz details, the support of France was essential in his election. In two other cases in the last 21 years the support of a major Northern power for an ostensible 'Third World' candidate for an executive-head post in the system was essential.

Brian
Urquhart

Erskine
Childers

A   WORLD   IN   NEED
OF   LEADERSHIP:
TOMORROW'S   UNITED   NATIONS
- A   FRESH   APPRAISAL -

may not be free to act in the best interests of the organization. Single terms of executive office would also remove this obstacle to eliminating mediocre or poor leadership in vital development and humanitarian work.

▶ Diplomatic delicacy

> Conduct which is wily and subtle, without being directly false or
> fraudulent, is styled 'diplomatic'.
> *Oxford English Dictionary for 1877.*

The basic delicacies of the diplomatic circuit also have a subtle influence on the process. An incumbent is often seen as 'one of us' who must not be 'insulted'; and thus even a demonstrably better new candidate may be viewed as an upstart outsider. The diplomatic community includes many people who find it difficult to perceive the deficiencies of an executive head as clearly as do those judging from the outside. The camaraderie of diplomatic life can soften the edges of critical judgment. This can be an important factor when the time comes to advise home governments as an executive head's term draws towards its close.

▶ Involvement of secretariat staff

The use of members of the Secretariat in promoting renewable terms is another factor in the present process. In a few worst cases Secretariat members have been instructed to campaign for the re-election of their executive head; in many, senior officers, having in mind the best chances for their own careers, do so even without any instruction. A conscientious ambassador, trying to assess the performance of the incumbent, may well try to obtain further insight by informal talks with well-placed staff members. If the staff member knows that the chief is bent on re-election— and has a good chance of getting it—he or she may well think twice about the danger of any criticism of the chief being quoted back to the front office.

▶ Inhibitions favouring re-eligibility

An important characteristic of renewable terms in any public service post, national or international, is the disinclination to give serious consideration to an alternative. The built-in advantage held by the incumbent is often at work before any alternative candidate is even in sight. In his numerous interviews with government representatives and others at FAO, Charles Weitz found 'widespread acknowledgement that the power of incumbency is such that unless a Director-General makes substantial errors of judgement, it would be difficult to unseat that incumbent if he or she stood for re-appointment'.

       The absence of clearly prescribed deadlines by which an incumbent must signify his or her intention can be powerfully worked to his advantage. Because of the 'delicacy' syndrome an incumbent who simply delays stating his intentions, one way or the other, can effectively stifle all movement about the post, even until quite shortly before it must be re-filled.

With or without such ploys the incumbency factor has been allowed to become far too dominant. It is all too easy for busy government officials in home capitals to shrug off as unrealistic all suggestions that there could be a change for the better; diplomats at the organization are reluctant even to speculate about what they regard as a futile exercise, lest any involvement may diminish their access to the incumbent in his presumed next term, or contravene casual acceptances of him uttered by their superiors at home.

The consequences of such forces and factors can often be the reappointment of incumbents about whom, if asked in total confidence, most delegates would voice criticisms that were quite enough to warrant a change. Indeed it has at times been astonishing to observe a kind of paralysis settling over the diplomatic community about an incumbent who had managed to provoke its virtually unanimous disapproval or lack of confidence a relatively short time before. Long-lasting damage has sometimes been done to a UN organization—to its reputation in the world at large, to its work, and to the morale of its staff—simply because, at the crucial moment, the incumbent seeking re-election had been afforded such formidable built-in advantages over any possible rival. It is essential to emphasise that all of this happens, not by any constitutional requirement but by the sheer ambivalence of governments. Their citizens, and the public at large, deserve better.

▶ The balance sheet

The case against renewability has been elaborated at some length because it is seldom thoroughly explored, whereas the arguments in favour of it are well known and ostensibly attractive. In strongly recommending the adoption of single terms this study's authors have no intention of belittling the record and memory of the fine leaders in the UN system who have served more than one term. The issue is whether the inherent dangers of renewability outweigh the benefits. In our view a longer term would ensure that the organization would receive an outstanding leader's best contributions, while protecting the system from the dangers of renewing terms of incumbents who were *not* outstanding.

The idea that an outstanding leader can make no further contribution except in continued service as an executive head in the UN system must also be questioned. In the early days when there were fewer UN organizations and a global agenda that posed far fewer simultaneous major challenges, this notion of total loss was strong. In a world that requires more and more complex multilateral machinery of varying kinds, including more and more regional mechanisms, the truly outstanding leader will always have opportunities to continue his or her public service internationally if not at home.

Brian
Urquhart

Erskine
Childers

A   W O R L D   I N   N E E D
O F   L E A D E R S H I P :
T O M O R R O W ' S   U N I T E D   N A T I O N S
– A   F R E S H   A P P R A I S A L –

The tradition of giving one member state a monopoly on a post is a powerful argument both against renewability and for an *end* to such monopolies.

The authors of this study believe that a standard rule of non-renewable terms of office, and a single seven-year term, would be highly desirable for the health of the UN system.

▶ Length of a single term

The relatively short length of terms in small and wholly technical agencies may make it desirable to maintain existing arrangements. The key issue to be addressed is the term of office of the Secretary-General and the executive heads of major entities of the UN system. The number of years should be long enough for an outstanding leader to make a decisive contribution and short enough for a less satisfactory incumbent not to do too much damage. Thus the inevitable possibility of error in selecting public leaders, even with the best possible process, will be limited.

Article 97 of the UN Charter says nothing at all about term of office of the Secretary-General, either as to renewability or length.

At Dumbarton Oaks the 'Sponsoring Governments' proposed a three-year term with re-election allowed (a British delegation cable back to London observed that a three-year term would make it possible 'to retain a suitable man indefinitely and dismiss a bad one within reasonable time'). This proposal was reluctantly accepted by the membership of the succeeding 1945 San Francisco UN Conference on International Organization (UNCIO)—but at a time when it was assumed that the Security Council's recommendation of a candidate to the General Assembly would be by a simple seven-member majority.

When, however, the USSR persuaded the other major powers that the veto provision in the Security Council should apply to recommendation of a candidate for Secretary-General, Committee I/2 went into reverse and insisted that length of term of office not be provided for in *any* way in the Charter. The delegations argued that the need for unanimous agreement among the permanent members of the Security Council to extend an incumbent every three years would either render the Secretary-General hopelessly subservient to them during such a short term, or result in his removal before being able to do a useful job. The Preparatory Commission recommended to the first General Assembly session that the *first* Secretary-General be appointed for a term of five years, 'the appointment being open at the end of that period for a further five-year term'.[29] At the first General Assembly session in London, this provision was adopted (Resolution II(1) of 24 January 1946).

There had not been much debate on all this at San Francisco, but Mexico offered alternative proposals for a single term of seven to ten years, and this affords a good starting point for examination of the question.

---

[29] Report of the UN Conference on International Organization (UNCIO), Doc. 1155, p. 2-4, and Report by the Executive Committee of the Preparatory Commission, Doc. PC/EX/113 Rev. 1, 12 November 1945.

The challenges that have always poured in upon the Secretary-General have no convenient timetables. The only sensible way to approach the question of length of a single term is therefore to judge the best period for a solid, valuable contribution, taking into account that this is a uniquely exhausting and debilitating job.

The Secretary-General and other major executive heads have usually needed about two years to assemble and organize a team of senior aides, to make the first vital rounds of capitals and regional or other group organizations, to steer a new medium-term programme of work through the governing organs, and to begin to make a substantial impression on the international community. With ongoing management duties and inevitable emergencies, it is usually about the third year before a Secretary-General emerges at full capacity.[30]

In the world of the 1990s and beyond, the immensely complex challenges of a more cohesive, multidisciplinary approach will have to be added to the leadership challenge. Future Secretaries-General will need to spend more time developing and consolidating their leadership of the UN system as a whole. Their colleagues in the agencies and programmes will need to spend comparable time adjusting to far more substantial coordination and mobilizing their respective constituencies.

Bearing all these challenges and responsibilities in mind, seven years seems a reasonable period for an effective single term for the Secretary-General and for the heads of at least the major agencies.

▶ Removal from office

Of the nearly thirty organizations covered in this study, a provision for removal from office formally exists at present in only six, all specialized agencies or voluntary funds.[31] Provisions for impeachment for grave dereliction of duty are standard in most national public structures, and poor performance of a Cabinet Minister in a parliamentary democracy almost invariably results in removal before long. Yet the UN system has no uniform provision for gross inadequacy or malfeasance in office.

To urge that provision for dereliction be made uniform throughout the system is in no way to imply that it has often been needed in the past; it has not. It is simply to suggest, again, that the United Nations system deserves the same protection against errors of judgment by electors or unexpected developments of personality that is regarded as vital in any sound national administration.

To avoid embarrassment governments should adopt provisions for removal from office uniformly throughout the UN system simultaneously with adjusting the term of office.

---

[30] In his FAO study Charles Weitz records the views of delegates during a debate on length of term which well illustrates what really happens for an executive head in a system that has biennial budgets: 'Again and again delegates had pointed out [that] a person elected for a four-year term must spend most of the first two years in office under a programme of work and budget of his predecessor.'

[31] UNESCO, WHO, UPU, ITU, WMO and IFAD.

VI.   FINDING THE BEST

The scope and quality of searching for the best possible candidates is important to all public service leadership posts. A shocking characteristic of the UN system to date has been the absence of this very concept and practice, and the resultant narrowness of the crucial preliminary process. There has been a tendency for candidates merely to appear from within a relatively circumscribed network of those already close to the organization, with a preponderance of self-promoted candidates, or sometimes candidates advanced by their governments.

A serious process of search is essential if the process of selection is to be improved and widened. This depends in the first place on enlarging the reservoir of candidates. This in turn depends on a number of factors, including the publishing of an impending vacancy and the perceived stature of both the organization and the job.

▶ Information about vacancies

> There is, of course, no advertisement for the post, no job description. To set
> out such priorities would be too political.
>
> *Sarah Helm* [32]

Vacancies in top public service posts in any democratic country become widely known through national media and political and professional organizations. Those of the UN system do not. The resources for UN system leadership, which by definition should be worldwide, are at present constricted from the outset.

The causes of this virtual silence about vacancies in top international positions include lack of interest in the international media. UN organizations are also to blame, because the vacancies are not posted and in most cases are not announced to the media in any positive way. Announcements of eligibility for reappointment of incumbents are not mandatory. The head of any organization who wishes to be re-elected is unlikely to make efforts to publish the vacancy concerned.

In their own countries governments are, by their own insistence, the prime agents of the UN system. This responsibility should include making UN vacancies known to the public, but this, too, has virtually never happened. Inevitably, therefore, information about vacancies becomes available only haphazardly, and only to 'inner circles' of diplomats and to specialized professional bodies in the case of the agencies.

It is sometimes argued that making these vacancies internationally 'transparent' might be

---

[32]   *The Independent*, 18 September 1991.

worse than the prevailing silence and might result in a flood of candidacies from all over the world, some manifestly unsuitable and implausible. But we have not reached the stage where these are in any sense popular elections. Basic information about the vacancies, including the simple fact that the posts are filled through government decisions, will deter the vast majority of 'nuisance' proposals; and governments can be counted upon to filter out aspirant citizens who would obviously prove nationally embarrassing. Above all, in a new age where the world is in need of courageous, imaginative leadership, limiting even the knowledge that UN leadership posts are becoming vacant makes no sense.

▶ *Image factors*

> The United Nations is pictured [in reporting] as a protagonist in a kind of global sporting event, which must either be won or lost in a given time. This makes for dramatic reading, but not for clear understanding. Such a view ignores the fact that crisis and difficulty are what the United Nations is for and that the game concerned is the endless drama of history itself.
>
> *Secretary-General U Thant, 1965* [33]

The popular image of the UN organization and of the job itself is another constraint upon the size of the reservoir of candidates. The UN, and much of the system, has been the subject of intensive criticism in recent years, some of it justified, much of it the result of shrewd efforts by some governments to make it the scapegoat for their own errors and of virulent extremist right-wing propaganda campaigns. Governments doing the scapegoating have, not surprisingly, been quite uninterested in correcting resultant meretricious media assaults on the UN; other governments which are perfectly aware of what has been going on have also remained silent.

If member governments display little interest in the UN, or participate in or remain silent over unwarranted attacks on it, the calibre of candidates coming forward for leadership positions is not likely to be high. The UN system unquestionably needs constructive criticism and monitoring. But a negative, or patronizing, or indifferent official attitude to the UN system will not attract the candidates for leadership which the situation demands and the international community deserves. The kind of superficial reporting which U Thant characterized thirty years ago is all too likely to make a vacant leadership post seem too problematic a career move to many potential candidates.

There is a direct correlation between the public perception of the worth of the UN system and the quality of the leadership it can aspire to. Such perceptions are formed by the UN system's secretariats, member governments, the media, and international and national non-governmental organizations (NGOs). More and more NGOs take very seriously the filling of key posts in

---

[33] Address to American Newspaper Publishers Convention, New York, 21 April 1965. UN Doc. SG/SM/283.

Brian
Urquhart

Erskine
Childers

A   WORLD   IN   NEED
OF   LEADERSHIP :
TOMORROW'S   UNITED   NATIONS
- A   FRESH   APPRAISAL -

countries, both in central political leadership and in specialized fields like environment and health. The increasingly shallow and mindlessly negative imagery currently projected about the UN system makes their vigilance all the more important to its future.

When, as the result of governmental inattention, an inadequate incumbent turns in a manifestly poor performance, this taints not only the organization concerned, but the post itself. A bad performance may well necessitate restoring the image of a post as part of the process of securing a first-rate replacement. Yet governments' expressed concern about a poor performance has by no means always carried forward into the successful installation of an outstanding replacement. Vigilance by all other actors in the international community is quite as necessary in such cases as in normal situations.

VII. SEARCHING

As already noted, a predominant tendency of the election or appointment process has been to consider only those who promote themselves, those who are promoted by one or more governments, or those who are already in the wings when compromise nominations are needed. This is not a search for candidates; it is merely sorting out pre-existing nominations from various sources.

The failure to provide for a serious search procedure has several causes. At the beginning there was an urgent need to get the new world organization started, and political conditions made a serious search procedure virtually impossible. The rise of permanent-mission, diplomatic communities at each UN headquarters generated the prevailing practice of leaving these matters increasingly to the members of these communities. The idea of renewability was reinforced by cases where it was known that an incumbent wanted another term.

As has been pointed out above, decisions to limit incumbents to one adequate term would obviously make a decisive change in this casual approach. But such a change should be complemented by adopting a properly prescribed and organized search process as part of the official appointment process.

Governments should adopt a uniform, common policy that a positive search process shall be a required preliminary for the selection of all executive heads in the UN system.

▶ Proper timetables

Few organizations in the UN system formally provide for the initiation of an election or appointment process on a specific timetable. The effectiveness of the timetables of some of those that have made such provisions has been doubtful. There is no such formal timetable even for the Secretary-Generalship, nor for any of the leadership posts which the Secretary-General fills by confirmation of the General Assembly.

As a crucial minimum improvement throughout the UN system for each appointment, dates should be established by which a proper search process must be launched. Such an opening date should be the first point in a prescribed timetable, which should include a date by which properly constituted nominations must be filed (closing of nominations), and a further date by which names of candidates must be circulated.[34]

---

[34] WHO's 1996 amendments clearly correct the deficiency that nominations had only been made available to its Executive Board on the opening day of the appointing session.

Brian
Urquhart

Erskine
Childers

A   W O R L D   I N   N E E D
O F   L E A D E R S H I P :
T O M O R R O W ' S   U N I T E D   N A T I O N S
- A   F R E S H   A P P R A I S A L -

▶ A system timetable?

> A cabinet is a combining committee—a hyphen which joins, a *buckle*
> which fastens the legislative part of the state to the executive part ...
> *Walter Bagehot, 1867* [35]

It has already been pointed out that there is absolutely no correlation between the year of appointment of a Secretary-General and that for any other post in the system. It is not that a new Secretary-General has to 'inherit' colleagues left over from a predecessor's team—the predecessor has had no role in forming *that* 'team' either.

The Secretary-General and the heads of the fifteen Specialized Agencies constitute the nearest thing the UN system has to an executive cabinet. A comparison with the fields of responsibility found in any national cabinet is not far-fetched. When the UN-system heads do meet around a table they represent the total concerns of humankind in Diplomacy, Security, Law,[36] Economy, Sustainable Development, Money and Finance, Trade, Labour and Employment, Agriculture, Industry, Education, Health, Telecommunications and Postal Services, Civil Aviation, Marine affairs, Meteorology, and Energy, to name only the major fields. It may be imagined how any national government would function if its chief executive could neither start a term of office with such a team freshly chosen, nor have any real say over who might later join it from one or another ministry.

A Secretary-General would, of course, not have the dilemmas posed by the need to reward faithful party service while at the same time seeking to assemble the best possible team. The main difficulty would be that the United Nations has no *legal* writ in any Specialized Agency, not even those whose name includes the words 'United Nations'. The Secretary-General could only suggest the most appropriate profile to those in an agency conducting a search in their own professional-technical terms. It is not intended to suggest that, like Prime Ministers, the incoming Secretary-General should choose the executive heads of the rest of the system; that would require major constitutional change in the system's structure. It can, however, be argued that it would not only help a new Secretary-General, but would help *governments* properly to fulfil their responsibilities for creating leadership and coherence in the system, if two improvements were brought about.

First, the calendar of executive-head appointments should be brought into alignment, so that all heads of the Specialized Agencies would be appointable early in the term of an incoming Secretary-General. This could be achieved by a system-wide agreement among member states— and they are the same member states—to re-phase the calendar of one term of office in each agency by minor abbreviation or extension.

---

[35] From essay on 'The Cabinet' in *The English Constitution*, 1867.
[36] The Secretary-General has a Legal Advisor and is responsible for the world depository of all treaties; the President of the World Court does not attend meetings of the UN-system 'cabinet', the ACC, but then nor do many Chief Justices attend national cabinets.

A new Secretary-General would need some time to identify new or adjusted UN-system strategies and priorities, and to test the views of the international community on these. He or she should also have time to appoint and draw on the advice of the Deputies earlier recommended. All of these desiderata, and the time for adequate searching, would indicate a re-alignment of Agency terms to commence at the beginning of the Secretary-General's second year. This would afford at least six years of a well-fashioned team.[37]

Secondly, by resolution in each governing body the new Secretary-General should be consulted on the selection of the next executive head of each Specialized Agency. By these means, without illicit interference, the Secretary-General could offer his or her opinion to the Agency appointive body on the mix of qualities needed over the forward period.

The foregoing proposed improvements do, of course, pre-suppose that selection of the Secretary-General would itself involve the improved criteria for inter-disciplinary team leadership, and the reorganization of the Office with Deputies that has been urged earlier in this study and elsewhere by the authors.

▶ Qualities and qualifications

Earlier in this study it was emphasised that, for the Secretary-Generalship, there is an important distinction between qualities and qualifications. It was noted that the UN Charter says very little about either, and what it does say is not very helpful. The authors of this study have suggested an outline list of the qualities needed for this extraordinary post. It has also been noted that the World Health Organization (WHO) has now actually adopted a set of criteria for its post of Director-General.

The WHO initiative demonstrates that it is perfectly possible for governments to agree on a short and general prescription of the minimal desiderata for leadership posts. This would have some definite benefits in imparting a certain stature and tone to the office concerned.

The General Assembly should adopt a statement of the basic qualities to be sought in a Secretary-General, and should invite all other governing bodies of the system to follow the example of the World Health Organization in this respect.

▶ Age criteria

The new and constantly expanding challenges to the UN system will call for extraordinary stamina in its leaders. There is now the additional consideration that humankind is maturing earlier, and that the population will be proportionally more youthful for many decades ahead. It is relevant to examine what the age-range of the executive leadership of the system has been.

---

[37] Although it is beyond the scope of this study it should be noted here that, for these and all other reasons, governments should also establish a common calendar for the medium-term programmes of the UN system and their indicative budgets. This was the original design for the system, when governments inscribed in the UN Charter that the General Assembly should review the budgets of the agencies.

Brian
Urquhart

Erskine
Childers

A   W O R L D   I N   N E E D
O F   L E A D E R S H I P :
T O M O R R O W ' S   U N I T E D   N A T I O N S
- A   F R E S H   A P P R A I S A L -

▶ **Table 6. Age of UN system executive heads**

Age at appoint-ment [1]	S-G's term in which appointment made								Age at end of term [2]	
	1946-52	1953-60	1961-71	1972-81	1982-1991	1992-	Total	per cent	Total	per cent
30's	1		1				2	1		
40's	5	4	3	8	5	4	29	19	6	5
50's	12	11	17	22	15	6	83	54	34	27
60's	9	3	7	5	8	6	38	24	66	54
70's	1		1	1			3	2	16	13
80's									1	1
Totals	28	18	29	36	28	16	155	100	123	100

[1] Multiple terms are not counted separately; see Table 8 for birth years and years of terms served.
[2] Excludes those currently holding another UN leadership post.

Only 19 per cent of executive heads in the system have been in their 40s when first appointed (Dag Hammarskjöld was 48 when he became Secretary-General). More than half of all executive heads of UN organizations have been newly appointed when in their fifties (54 per cent), including three Secretaries-General, Trygve Lie at 50, Kurt Waldheim at 54, and U Thant at 52. Two Secretaries-General have been appointed in their 60s, Javier Pérez de Cuellar at 62 and Boutros Boutros-Ghali at 69. Of all executive heads 54 per cent have served until they were in their sixties. The two heads appointed in their thirties were Eric White, who then spent 20 years as the head of GATT, and Sadruddin Aga Khan as UN High Commissioner for Refugees.

The proportions of appointment in different age-decades have not significantly shifted over the fifty years except for a decline in the number who began in their 70s, chiefly elder statesmen in the early years. The number who end their terms in their 70s (13.7 per cent over the total period) clearly reflects the unlimited renewability of terms of office discussed earlier.

In the year 2000 half the world's population, some 3 billion people, will be under age 25. While no dogmatic age-criteria should be laid down, it is obvious that posts like that of Secretary-General call for extraordinary stamina. If properly assisted by, and properly delegating to, outstanding Deputies as recommended in this and the authors' associated studies, a Secretary-General may be relieved at least of some of the physical and mental strain that less well organized UN heads have imposed on themselves.

Secretaries-General, and indeed a number of other executive heads in the system must be able to reach out to young people, gain their confidence, and motivate them. This is not impossible for older people but it is a quality that should be carefully considered in looking at candidates. In this and in all respects, the future leaders of the international system should be at the height of their powers and ability to communicate, in order to shoulder the demanding daily workload and the public responsibilities that a different and highly complex world is going to expect of them.

▶ Gender criteria

The gender record of UN system leadership so far elected and appointed by governments is appalling, especially in view of the affirmative and egalitarian provisions of the UN Charter, human rights declarations, conventions and resolutions.

Even in the mid-1990s, after decades of legal instruments and exhortations and four UN world conferences on women, the deplorable fact is that, out of 155 executive-head posts in the UN system itself, only 5 have been held by women. They are in fact five executive heads out of 26 in office in 1996. This heroic 19 per cent achievement in gender equity is not, however, as significant as the surface arithmetic may suggest. All five women are heading UN voluntarily-financed development and humanitarian funds (UNEP, UNFPA, UNHCR, UNICEF and WFP)—all appointed, not elected positions. Governments have never to date elected a woman to head a Specialized Agency.

Advances have indeed been made in gender-balanced initial, and to some extent mid-level, recruitment, but the effect of this is many years away up promotion ladders, and in any case would not often affect executive-head positions.

Secretaries-General and other executive heads have not used their special appointment capabilities to ensure a remotely acceptable proportion of women in senior-echelon posts. It is essential that a much greater effort be made to ensure that women should have fully equal opportunity for all UN leadership posts. Governments themselves, of course, have a very long way to go to provide an example among themselves even at the UN: not even 5 per cent of the 185 Permanent Representatives currently assigned to the United Nations by governments are women.

If the UN's own decisions are any guide, necessary affirmative provisions to ensure equal opportunity, in line with existing UN system legislation regarding the UN civil service, should provide that 50 per cent of the candidates for executive-head posts finally assembled in each organization's short list should be women.

It would be very healthy for the United Nations and for the system as a whole if the next Secretary-General were a woman.

▶ Discussing the next leadership

No organization in the UN system presently requires any kind of discussion of the desirable nature of future leadership. With their new procedure for substantive screening of a short list of candidates, members of the WHO Executive Board might hold such a discussion before the interviews—as it were, reviewing the implications of the basic criteria now established in terms of the health needs of the international community in the period ahead. But this is not prescribed.

Ideally there should be a discussion of future leadership requirements by delegations and it should be rendered into a consensus document. Given the ongoing disagreements on major

Brian
Urquhart

Erskine
Childers

A   WORLD   IN   NEED
OF   LEADERSHIP:
TOMORROW'S   UNITED   NATIONS
-A   FRESH   APPRAISAL-

aspects of global policy and agenda, this may not be possible. This should not, however, inhibit discussion of the subject.

As it is widely recognized that the UN system must develop far greater public understanding and support, the views of the non-governmental community about future leadership should also be obtained.

As an illustration of what should be possible, on the eve of the appointment year for Secretary-General the General Assembly would conduct a discussion of the requirements of future leadership, beginning with public hearings.[38] Members of the Security Council would automatically be present. Staff of the Search secretariat, who should already have been assigned and be preparing for their work, would monitor the discussion. The views expressed should be available in printed record for the benefit of the public.

There might be some initial sensitivity over whether such a discussion might be 'disrespectful' of the outgoing Secretary-General. If that incumbent has been of adequate stature there should be no reason for such constraint, especially with the ending of renewable terms; the discussion would be about the future. In a world where millions still barely survive in misery, choosing its chief public servant is far too important a matter to be constrained by artificial delicacies from a bygone diplomatic age.

As a preliminary to a new appointment process the full-membership deliberative body of each organization of the system should hold a discussion of the kind of leadership that will be needed in the coming years. Such discussions should be conducted in open session, and the proceedings should be available to the public. The intergovernmental discussion should be preceded by public hearings.

▶ *The search process*

Outstanding potential leaders do not automatically become known in the right place at the right time. If Dag Hammarskjöld's name had not occurred to one ambassador at the right time, or if that ambassador had for some reason been absent, it is almost certain that he would never have become Secretary-General. The need for and purposes of a properly organised search process have been discussed earlier. It should comprise two elements, one continuous, the other specific to each election period.

The senior official responsible for personnel matters in each organization should be specifically charged with assembling and maintaining a well-researched list of outstanding leadership talent for *all* senior posts up to and including the executive head (i.e., a pool of 'talent to watch', not just for the very next vacancy).

---

[38] This is no longer as outlandish an idea as it might have seemed even a few years ago. In 1994 the President of the General Assembly conducted four days of 'World Hearings on Development' at which heads of institutes and individuals presented their views and discussed with delegations an agenda for development.

This list would only be a starting point for the actual search process and would have no larger objective or status. The list would simply be made available as source material for the pre-election search.

▶ *Search committees: elected heads*

For each vacancy that is filled by an actual election, a special search committee or group should be established by the relevant intergovernmental organ, on a balanced geographical basis. This may itself be intergovernmental, or a special group of eminent persons outside of either government or the UN system.

In the case of the UN Secretary-Generalship, this committee or group would be established by the Security Council which, under Article 97 of the Charter, has the prerogative of recommending a candidate to the General Assembly. It would be proper for the Council to consult with the President of the General Assembly on the composition of the Search Committee. The Search Committee would, of course, comprise both permanent and non-permanent members. In the specialized agencies, member governments might decide that the search committee would be constituted by the Executive Board or Council. Reasonably compact size would be essential.

It is, of course, possible that tensions such as those between North and South and between major powers and the majority of member states might hamper the working of an intergovernmental search body, especially for the UN Secretary-Generalship. It is suggested by some that the same tendencies towards 'deals' and the same kinds of pressures as in its parent body would hamper the work of any such search body. The obvious question then is, if it is accepted that a search process is essential, how else and by whom might it be carried out on behalf of governments?

The alternative is that the appropriate standing body of the organization appoints a representative group of eminent and manifestly disinterested persons to conduct the actual search on its behalf and under its aegis.

In many respects this would be a better instrument. Such a group of men and women could be assembled from among the leaders in the relevant disciplines. They could include former heads or ministers of government, veteran diplomats, noted academicians, business leaders, and other highly respected public figures chosen for their objectivity. A search by such a group would have the world public's confidence and respect. It would, indeed, enhance the stature of the Office of Secretary-General of the United Nations, as would the equivalent search group the stature of the other executive offices in the system. The fact that there has been no movement towards even intergovernmental searches suggests this alternative should be considered.

Again to take the Secretary-Generalship as the example, such a search group would work in complete confidentiality under the Security Council, making periodic progress reports to it. The group would be charged with assembling the short list which has earlier been recommended, 71

Brian
Urquhart

Erskine
Childers

*A WORLD IN NEED
OF LEADERSHIP:
TOMORROW'S UNITED NATIONS
- A FRESH APPRAISAL -*

and which the Council would then make public at mid-point for comment, without being under any formal obligation to accept those names. The group would be dissolved before the Council undertook its final procedures to choose, from its or an adjusted short list, the single candidate to be recommended to the General Assembly.

In Specialized Agencies preferring the same alternative (and with equivalent benefits), such a search group would submit its recommendations to the established electoral machinery of the organization concerned.

As with all recommendations for improvements in this study, the ultimate decisions and choice of options lie with member governments, with whatever advice others who influence them may offer. These, however, would seem to be the only two acceptable options. The continuation of the present non-process, in which there is no effective search at all, is no longer acceptable.

These are, after all, essential jobs as far as the future and welfare of humankind are concerned. Presumably, therefore, they warrant a considerable and serious effort to find the best possible candidates.

▶ The nature of the search

On the basis of single terms of seven years, the search period could begin eighteen months before the election or appointment of the Secretary-General, or of executive heads in other organizations. The absolute minimum feasible would be for the search process to be fully operational as of the first day of the year at the end of which a Secretary-General would be appointed. An equivalent minimum period should apply in Specialized Agencies.

The search committees should be given a wide mandate. They should be able to consult with whomsoever they judge useful—regional groups, individual governments, the outgoing executive head and predecessors, senior members of the Secretariat, institutes and non-governmental organizations. They would undoubtedly consult eminent figures in fields related to the organization's tasks. They should be equipped to carry out confidential research on the qualifications, working record and personal suitability of potential candidates; to interview candidates; and in all other ways to conduct their search throughout the prescribed period until satisfied that they have made a sound international canvassing of available talent. Budgetary provision should be made for travel and adequate supporting staff of high quality.

The proposed organization of a search is a modest improvement, given the global and ever more complex responsibilities of the leadership of the UN system. Indeed there is no serious excuse for its absence. Equivalent leadership posts in nation states may be filled through the rough and tumble of politics; but the UN system's leadership is not subject to the rise and fall of democratically-governed cabinets or other national political changes; it is entirely amenable to the kind of search process that is mandatory in virtually all important public and corporate institutions, including international ones.

▶ Judicial examples

> The parliamentary assembly votes with absolutely no knowledge of the
> candidate proposed. We have never met him, heard of him or know
> anything about him.
>> *Lord Kirkhill, 1996, on appointments to the Court of Human Rights* [39]

In 1996 the Council of Europe adopted improved procedures for the selection of Judges of the European Court of Human Rights, following criticism that members of the appointing Parliamentary Assembly of the Council seldom knew anything about the candidates for whom they had to vote. Beginning in 1997 all candidates for judgeships on the new consolidated Court of Human Rights must complete proper *curricula vitae*, and will be interviewed and assessed by a subcommittee of the assembly.

A long-standing exception to the generally casual approach to appointments in the UN system is the procedure for search and selection of its judicial arm. Candidates for the fifteen judgeships of the International Court of Justice are nominated by government-appointed national groups of known experts in international law. Only nominations that satisfy the highest standards set by their peers can qualify for consideration by both the General Assembly and the Security Council in separately held, absolute-majority elections. The Judges then elect the President and Vice-President of the Court.

▶ Search systems for appointed heads

The process of appointing the executive heads of the UN funds and programmes is different from both the Secretary-Generalship and the Specialized Agencies and requires separate treatment.

These are special-purpose entities established by the General Assembly and financed in whole or largely by voluntarily contributed ('extra-budgetary') contributions. They have their own governing bodies elected by the Economic and Social Council and composed of representatives of member states. Their executive heads, however, are all appointed by the Secretary-General except that the head of the World Food Programme is appointed in consultation with the head of FAO, and the head of the UN University with the head of UNESCO. The terms of office vary from three to five years. All are renewable without any prescribed limit as to the number of terms.

---

[39] The rapporteur of the Parliamentary Assembly of the Council of Europe, quoted in *The European*, 25 April–1 May 1996, on the eve of the changes noted above.

Brian
Urquhart

Erskine
Childers

A   W O R L D   I N   N E E D
O F   L E A D E R S H I P :
T O M O R R O W ' S   U N I T E D   N A T I O N S
- A   F R E S H   A P P R A I S A L -

▶ **Table 7. Appointed executive head posts: selection procedures[1]**

| Organ | Term of office | | | | Procedures for selection | | |
	Years	No. of terms	Time-table	Nomina-tion by	Search	Scrutiny	Confirm
UNCHS	Unsp[2]	No limit	No	S-G	No	None[3]	UN GA
UNCTAD	Unsp	No limit	No	S-G	No	None	UN GA
UNDP	4	No limit	No	S-G	No	None	UN GA
UNEP	4	No limit	No	S-G	No	None	UN GA
UNFPA	4	No limit	No	S-G	No	None	UN GA
UNHCR	5	No limit	No	S-G	No	None	UN GA
UNICEF	5	No limit	No	S-G	No	None	UN GA
UNRWA	3	No limit	No	S-G	No	Yes[4]	UN GA
UNU	5	Two	Yes	Comm.	Yes[5]	Yes	S-G/D-G
WFP	5	No limit	No	S-G/D-G	No	None	UN GA

[1] This table treats posts of executive heads who are appointed by the UN Secretary-General (in some instances in consultation with another executive head), such appointment then only being confirmed by an intergovernmental body. For definitions of column headings see Table 5, page 46.
[2] Length of term unspecified; decided by the Secretary-General.
[3] The 'consultation' informally carried out by the Secretary-General with members of the various governing bodies of these funds/programmes cannot be described as scrutiny or screening, hence the negative entry for most.
[4] The Advisory Committee of UNRWA does act as a scrutinising and screening body, and recommends a candidate to the Secretary-General.
[5] An actual Search Committee was established in 1996 for the next appointment of Rector of the University.

All require exceptionally talented and experienced leadership. The heads of the United Nations Development Programme (UNDP), Children's Fund (UNICEF), Population Fund (UNFPA) and World Food Programme (WFP) alone are responsible for thousands of development projects in developing countries; the world-wide volume of displaced persons of all categories now confronting the office of the High Commissioner for Refugees (UNHCR) exceeds 40 million. The UN Environment Programme (UNEP) and the UN Centre for Human Settlements (UNCHS) address highly technical worldwide problems. Nonetheless, although their leaders' appointment by the Secretary-General should make it easier to conduct proper search and selection processes, Table 7 shows serious deficiencies.

▶ *Present practice*

There are no rules for nominations for these posts other than for the UN University (UNU), or guidelines for the requisite qualifications or experience of candidates.[40] No organized search is carried out by the Secretary-General or any representative body except, for the first time, by the

---

[40] A Search Committee, so entitled, was advertising and inviting applications and relative proposals in the Spring of 1996 for a final nomination for the next Rector in 1997.

UN University in 1996. Otherwise, candidates simply materialize. No governing body normally meets to consider an appointment except in the case of the UNU whose Council approves a short list of nominations from which the Secretary-General chooses with the concurrence of the Director-General of UNESCO. There is an unwritten tradition that the heads of UNDP and UNICEF should be U.S. nationals. In the case of UNDP the United States has always simply sent the Secretary-General the name; candidatures for UNICEF have recently at least included European challengers.

The Secretary-General does 'consult' members of the governing body, nominally if there is really only one name, rather more if there are several. General Assembly rubber-stamp confirmation of the appointment follows. Of the eleven executive heads to date in UNDP, UNICEF and UNFPA—organizations which exist exclusively to assist developing countries— only four had prior working experience in Third World development. Only two of these (both heading UNFPA) have been nationals of developing countries. Only two of the eleven incumbents have been women.[41]

The appointed heads then all seek high visibility because governments expect them to raise large sums of money every year in direct competition with each other and with bilateral agencies (while the same governments demand 'better coordination'). The law of advantage of incumbency not surprisingly works well here; the tendency to re-appoint seems to have become nearly automatic, partly also because terms of office are short.

▶ *Improvements*

The authors have recommended elsewhere that the development funds on one hand, and the humanitarian arms of the system on the other, should be consolidated for greater effectiveness and economies of overheads.[42] From such re-structuring there would be:

► a single UN Development Authority (consolidating UNDP, UNFPA, UNICEF and smaller development funds) headed by a Deputy Secretary-General for International Economic Co-operation and Sustainable Development and assisted by an Administrator of the Development Authority. There should be a single global governing body for periodic policy and accountability and regional governing bodies for programmes in each region.
► a single organization for humanitarian emergency operations consolidating WFP's food-aid operations and UNICEF's relief functions with the UN Department of Humanitarian Affairs, also headed by a Deputy Secretary-General. UNHCR would revert to its original refugee-protection roles.

---

[41] Nafis Sadik of UNFPA and, since 1995, Carol Bellamy in the Children's Fund after it had been headed by men for 48 years.
[42] See Childers with Urquhart, *Renewing the United Nations System, op. cit.*

Brian
Urquhart

Erskine
Childers

A   WORLD   IN   NEED
OF   LEADERSHIP:
TOMORROW'S   UNITED   NATIONS
- A   FRESH   APPRAISAL -

For the thus reduced total number of executive heads of special-purpose funds under the authority of the Secretary-General, a single term of seven years should also be instituted.

The recommended consolidations would greatly simplify executive-head appointments in the UN, but the selection process should nonetheless measure up to the responsibilities and the complexity of the work. The Secretary-General should be assisted by publicly announced search panels including eminent specialists in the relevant field.

▶ National monopoly

The tradition of a major contributor, the United States, having a permanent monopoly of the leadership of certain UN funds and programmes has ceased to have any even pragmatic justification. Other donor governments now make contributions as large, even in straight dollar volume; in per capita terms more than ten governments contribute so much more as to place the 'single largest donor' far down such a per capita list. Any monopoly inherently and severely limits the Secretary-General's responsibility, derogates from that Office, and reduces the General Assembly's 'confirmation' to a ritual, because all governments assume that the Secretary-General is simply handed a nomination by the government concerned. Furthermore, the practice of national monopolies on any senior-official posts has been expressly prohibited by General Assembly resolution.[43]

The Secretary-General should implement this resolution, making it known that no member state has any monopoly on any of the executive-head posts in UN funds, and that they will be filled by the very best qualified persons available.

---

[43] General Assembly resolution 35/210 of 17 December 1980: 'no post should be considered the exclusive preserve of any Member State or group of Member States'. This resolution has been reiterated in subsequent years.

VIII.   EXAMINING THE CANDIDATES

The Secretary-Generalship and, in appropriate degree, the leadership of other major organizations, require both dynamic and public leadership ability and the capacity for imaginative teamwork on complex problems. Neither of these critically important qualities is easily identified from a *curriculum vitae*. It is also axiomatic that personal qualities, dedication and commitment, and reasonable rather than excessive self-confidence, are only revealed in direct encounters.

Candidates on a short list produced by the search process should be further examined by the governing bodies. They should be invited to spend some hours discussing their analysis of challenges to be addressed, and their approach to such tasks, with an appropriately limited panel. For the Secretary-Generalship, this would be the Security Council itself. For funds and programmes it should be a suitable mechanism of the governing body. In many Agencies it could be the Council or Board, as is now to be the procedure in WHO. These proceedings should be accessible to the public either directly or by availability of transcripts.

In his conclusions to his study of FAO Charles Weitz offers an interesting alternative formula

> to try to 'equalize the playing field' by organizing, at the headquarters and at each regional location, a public appearance for the candidates where each would make an oral presentation and each would answer questions put by a panel of eminent outside persons. The transcript of these presentations could be circulated in all official languages to member governments and to an agreed list of universities, research institutions, NGOs and other sites.

Would top-calibre leaders, especially for the post of Secretary-General but also for agencies, be willing to submit themselves to one or the other variant on such scrutiny? For example, would the Prime Minister of a country consent to be interviewed by the Security Council, or refuse for fear of loss of his or her dignity or the political consequences at home should she or he not secure the nomination?

The office of the Secretary-General of the United Nations has, since World War II, been the highest international office in the world. If enough governments now act in time to prevent the United Nations from being closed down through imposed bankruptcy or otherwise destroyed by its ideological antagonists, this office should become increasingly visible and important to the international community. The future leadership of the United Nations system is an extremely important matter. Although currently threatened by a powerful minority, the United Nations is now more broadly understood worldwide as a vital

Brian
Urquhart

Erskine
Childers

A WORLD IN NEED
OF LEADERSHIP:
TOMORROW'S UNITED NATIONS
- A FRESH APPRAISAL -

element in a very troubled world. Those who aspire to lead it should surely be ready to present themselves and their ideas to its representatives.

The fear of being rejected should not discourage candidates who may be politically active in their own country. It would be virtually impossible to keep the candidacy of, say, a Prime Minister for the Secretary-Generalship, or of an Agriculture Minister for head of FAO, secret from the media. The proposed search process, which would be likely to remain discreet at the early investigative stages, should afford a would-be candidate of high national stature the opportunity to make a realistic assessment of his or her chances before assenting to the possible risks of meeting with the interviewing group.

Such an invitation, whatever the outcome, should be seen as a tribute to the person concerned.

IX. CAMPAIGNING FOR OFFICES

Active individual campaigning for nomination, a practice unheard of in the UN until 1970, should be unacceptable. In some of the Specialized Agencies, comparable behaviour has been allowed to develop. There are two prevalent forms of campaigning: by people outside the UN system, and by serving Secretariat members.

▶ *Campaigning from the outside*

The time may come when the Secretary-General is elected by some more directly popular machinery than by member-governments alone. At that time it might be appropriate for would-be candidates actively to put themselves forward for public scrutiny. That day has not yet arrived.

Until such fundamental changes come about, the arguments against active campaigning are conclusive. The first is one of equity: candidates from more affluent governments or backgrounds have an automatic advantage. The costs of campaigning are obvious—for example, staying in New York for recurring periods before the year of election to be seen and heard and to entertain, and travel to important capitals. Charles Weitz, describing the advent in FAO elections of full-scale political campaigning, poses the essential question:

> How are member states to judge fairly when one candidate has access to the equivalent of a multi-million dollar fund to print brochures, travel with the limit only of time and stamina, hold dinners [and] involve financial incentives ... while another candidate who may be equally well qualified may have only travel ability [on] a national airline and only such hospitality as local missions can divert from their limited representational funds?

Campaigning with the support of a government, which has been common practice in recent times, is related to the first issue. A candidate who secures support from an affluent government has an advantage that may have little to do with his or her qualifications for the job. Potentially excellent candidates may well be people who would not dream of campaigning at all. The decisive argument against campaigning, however, is that it will be virtually impossible for the ultimate electors to know what may already have been promised during such campaigning—for example, senior secretariat posts promised to governments in return for their support. Other bargains, future compromises, intimations or assurances of important policy positions, will also not be known. These considerations are not theoretical.

There is no possible way of ensuring against such infringements of candidates' impartiality, objectivity or independence except to end campaigning. Candidates who campaign for an office should be excluded from consideration. This rule should apply throughout the UN system for all executive head posts without exception. Campaigning cannot be concealed for

Brian
Urquhart

Erskine
Childers

A   W O R L D   I N   N E E D
O F   L E A D E R S H I P :
T O M O R R O W ' S   U N I T E D   N A T I O N S
– A   F R E S H   A P P R A I S A L –

long, and search committees and panels will know of such activity. If it is clearly stated that search groups will not include in their lists anyone they judge to be campaigning, the practice will quite quickly cease.

▶ Civil servant candidates

The practice of campaigning has also extended into the ranks of the UN civil service. Here, of course, it can be less obvious: the person is already in the circuit, in contact with national diplomats in connection with his work, even with officials in capitals while on official travels for the organization. Such campaigners have usually been senior civil servants and are thus well placed to campaign during what appear to be their normal duties. They also have the opportunities to get other staff to campaign for them, under a threat that need scarcely be voiced—that if they are elected, it will go hard for any career civil servant known either to have refused such assistance or to have opposed them. Even if not elected, recalcitrant staff members may suffer the consequences of lack of cooperation.[44]

Such abuses of UN civil service conduct are the consequence of permitting the practice of campaigning at all. It may well be that on occasion the best possible next executive head might be someone from within the ranks of the organization. If campaigning by staff members is tolerated, the staff member who refuses to campaign but who deserves to be considered will be at a major disadvantage, however honourable his or her conduct may be. Such an undesirable situation can only be avoided by a clear proscription of all campaigning. Again, an efficient search body will have little difficulty in learning of violations of such a rule. In addition, the relevant Staff Regulations should make an explicit provision that international civil servants in the UN system, while fully eligible for consideration as candidates for the leadership posts, must refrain from any campaigning activity to advance themselves.

▶   Campaigning for any executive-head post in the UN system should result in disqualification from that or any future candidature, and removal from office if proved after election. Staff of an organization should be eligible for consideration but the same prohibition on campaigning must apply.

The analysis made in foregoing pages covers the essential problems, weaknesses and remedies needed in the present procedures for the election and appointment of the top leadership of the UN system. The recommendations made will be assembled at the end of this study as its conclusions. There is, however, a tier of leadership immediately below that of the executive heads that is of critical importance. It consists of those most senior staff, in posts subject to the direct personal (often called 'political') appointment of the executive head, who constitute each organization's senior echelon.

---

[44]   Charles Weitz records in his study that, 'Much of the controversy which has swirled around past [FAO] elections, in particular those of 1967, 1971, and 1993, has concerned treatment of staff who were contesting'.

The quality and organization of these senior echelons, and their day to day leadership of the staff on behalf of the executive head, both reflect and significantly condition the effectiveness of an incumbent. So important are they in what ultimately makes for outstanding or indifferent leadership in the system that the manner of their appointment must be treated here.

X. APPOINTMENTS TO THE SENIOR ECHELON

The present senior echelon in the UN Secretariat consists of some 30-40 Under Secretaries-General (USG),[45] Assistant Secretaries-General (ASG) and senior Directors (D-2) under them heading divisions in departments. Except for those who carry out diplomatic or 'special representative' functions for the Secretary-General, the USG-ASG senior echelon consists mainly of the operational heads of departments. These senior officers are responsible for implementing all the work programmes of the UN, for effectively using its budget, and for ensuring the quality, direction and morale of its international civil service staff.

Comparable senior echelons exist in all other organizations of the system, though the number of officers with USG rank is proportionately fewer not only because of overall size of establishments but because other executive heads do not have the same need of short-term Special Representatives.

These senior staff have critically important functions. Under the Charter, appointments to the senior echelon as to all other staff positions are supposed to be the exclusive personal responsibility of the Secretary-General. Comparable provisions exist in the constitutions of agencies. Governments undertake to respect the secretariats' 'exclusively international character', and the paramount staffing considerations are to be 'the necessity of securing the highest standards of efficiency, competence, and integrity'.[46]

In the United Nations, however, by an early 'gentleman's agreement' five of the original eight Assistant Secretaries-General were to be nationals of the five permanent members of the Security Council and virtually chosen by them.[47] This introduced into the Secretariat from the outset an element of privileged national representation, and abridged the Charter's explicit provisions. With this example from the 'permanent five', not surprisingly other governments with one or another kind of special leverage have pressed for favoured nationals to be recruited into senior posts. The disease also spread laterally in the system.

While some of these privileged members of the senior echelon have proven outstanding, many have been only average or even inferior. Many others in the senior echelon have, of course, been personally selected by Secretaries-General for given jobs, but by no means all of these had the requisite qualifications either.

This senior UN echelon has responsibilities at a very high level, yet very few reach these top positions through UN civil service performance and promotion procedures. Only a few have risen through the ranks and professional testing of the Secretariat to this echelon. For these jobs

---

[45] The number of USGs, in particular, among these three ranks fluctuates considerably because the rank is given to the 'Special Representatives of the Secretary-General' who are assigned to crises and other temporary tasks.

[46] Charter Articles 100 and 101.

[47] Originally there were no Under Secretaries-General (USG); the highest rank, immediately below Secretary-General, was ASG.

no vacancy is published nor job description gazetted, and the normal procedures for recruitment and appointment do not apply. Vacancies are the focus of jockeying and diplomatic lobbying. The psychology of the re-eligibility of a Secretary-General, discussed earlier, has also played its part in denying the Secretariat 'only the very best'. The incumbents are not accountable to a periodic performance review process or monitoring body of any kind.

▶ The cascade effect

The arrival of a dynamic and pre-eminently qualified executive head at a UN-system organization can have an instantly positive chain-effect downwards on the staff as a whole, beginning with the senior echelon which manages it. The good executive head will choose and assign members of the senior echelon with care; ensure that they carry out their management, recruitment and promotion responsibilities scrupulously; and do their best to weed out (or render harmless) any inherited mediocrity in these salient posts. Morale rises. The sense of being privileged to work in the UN system strengthens integrity, innovation, and productivity.

The *converse* cascade effect, however, is equally rapidly felt from a mediocre or inadequate executive head who does not take adequate care over the quality and organization of the senior echelon. Morale ebbs. Inadequate managers deprive staff of leadership and direction. Good staff are inappropriately assigned or tasked so that they may seem to be 'deadwood'. Staff are mindlessly shuffled sideways into vacancies in expanding units for which they are totally unsuitable, stultifying new and often high-priority programmes. Recruitment and promotion become subject to political pressures and favouritism, with grave consequences for years to come.

The adverse cascade effect has happened too often. Member governments, whose delegations spend so much time and energy elaborating (some say micro-managing) the UN's actual work programmes, bear heavy responsibility for this state of affairs. They devote extraordinarily little time or energy to ensuring that these programmes will be executed by the best possible managers. While the paramount key in this is governments' choice of executive heads, far more care needs to be taken over the senior echelon as well.

▶ Improvements

USGs, ASGs and D-2s must, of course, continue to be appointed by the Secretary-General. Their selection, however, must be demystified and given a level of attention commensurate with their responsibilities. The Secretary-General—one of whose indispensable qualifications should be the ability to lead the staff—should be freed from corridor manoeuvering, pressure and lobbying. He or she should be protected from pressures to shuffle staff indiscriminately, or to recruit retiring diplomats or others lacking the necessary qualifications (or lacking the necessary superior skill in them).

Brian
Urquhart

Erskine
Childers

*A WORLD IN NEED
OF LEADERSHIP :
TOMORROW'S UNITED NATIONS
- A FRESH APPRAISAL -*

The Secretary-General should be discouraged from making indifferent choices in the senior echelon, should be helped to make the best possible choices, and must be able to work through the best possible organization of the top of the house.

The General Assembly should *decide* on the basic organization of the top of the Secretariat, establishing the posts of Deputy Secretary-General to head consolidated departments.

In the same resolution the General Assembly should further *decide* that all vacancies for senior-echelon posts should be publicly announced and that all positions in the Secretariat including all USG, ASG and D-2 posts should carry properly prepared and gazetted job descriptions, with the necessary indications to maintain the general geographical and gender balance of the top echelon. The General Assembly should require that each announcement of an appointment in the senior echelon shall describe the appointee's qualifications *in relation to the responsibilities of that specific post*. This would greatly help to discourage the long-evident phenomenon of unsuitable and substandard appointments.

The Secretary-General should implement the General Assembly provision against national monopolies on senior posts, and the Assembly should hold him or her accountable in this. The General Assembly should introduce measures to discourage a member state from supplementing UN remuneration of its nationals in the secretariat. It should also remedy the conditions which have motivated this practice in the past.

The equivalent practices should be standard in all other parts of the UN system, in order to bring the system's entire combined senior echelon up to the highest possible levels of quality and appropriateness for these responsibilities. The recommended United Nations System Consultative Board should commission a periodic independent review and evaluation of this echelon, with report to all governing bodies.

The Directors of Human Resources and Management (or Personnel) should maintain well researched lists of top-calibre potential candidates. The Director, or a senior official designated by the Secretary-General or other executive head, should interview candidates, seek independent outside views on their suitability, and in all such ways ensure that there can be no excuse of unavailability of persons of the requisite calibre and qualifications.

CHAPTER THREE

CONCLUSIONS AND RECOMMENDATIONS

I.   CONCLUSIONS

> No duty the Executive had to perform was so trying as to put the right man
> in the right place.
>
> *Thomas Jefferson* [48]

It is indeed not easy to make sound appointments, even from the reservoir of talent within a single culture and when those selecting are a closely related group. That from 51 to now 185 governments from every corner of Earth have managed to agree at all on whom to elect or appoint to the leadership of the United Nations system every five years or so is no small accomplishment.

If this study has been critical about these processes, however, it has been because the conditions that would make the choice easier for governments, and ensure that the chosen were of the highest quality, have not been in place.

The study does not suggest strange or exotic new procedures for search, screening, election and appointment. Its recommendations are all quite mundane, drawn from well-tested experience in a wide variety of institutions throughout the world. It bears repeating that the smallest academic institution or well-established corporation virtually anywhere in the world devotes far more time, energy and systematic effort to searching for its executive head than do governments for the Secretary-General of the United Nations.

It is true that the United Nations is subject, in these issues, to political considerations and especially to the politics of major powers, and that the presence of a veto-power over selection of a candidate for Secretary-General has had an inherently distorting effect on the process of choice. This should not mean, however, that the process of finding the best person to be the highest and most universally responsible public servant in the world should forever be handicapped. If all concerned can perceive that needs that are in reality in the common interest are not being adequately met, there can be change, provided, of course, that governments really want a more effective international system. The United Nations system itself has, after all, been the crucible for a series of remarkable changes in the behaviour of governments.

It has seldom been easy to secure the attention and interest of member governments to the Specialized Agencies' periodic needs for renewal of their executive heads. There are different levels of perception of the importance of the agencies, and their links to the central offices of government are often tenuous. Yet again and again, when the need has arisen, the attention of the necessary branches of government has been secured, enabling the Agencies to move effectively.

---

[48]   The third President of the United States, quoted in J.B. MacMaster, *History of the People of the United States* (1883-1913), Vol. 2, Ch. 13, page 586

Brian
Urquhart

Erskine
Childers

A   WORLD   IN   NEED
OF   LEADERSHIP:
TOMORROW'S   UNITED   NATIONS
- A   FRESH   APPRAISAL -

The needs and problems addressed in this study are not of such overwhelming complexity as to defy the proven capability of governments to make changes and improvements. The United Nations system, by its nature, is more dependent upon the quality of its human resources than any other public-service institution. It has none of the classic assets of national public-service institutions—no economic assets, no military or political power of its own, no territory beyond its headquarters buildings. It has only the basic importance of its principles and goals, the validity and momentum of its mandates, and the capability of its staff. The articulation of the system's goals, the implementation of its mandates, and the effective use of its staff depend in first instance on its executive leaders. This study has not sought perfection in the finding of such leaders, which is obviously unattainable. It has rather tried to identify better ways to achieve more consistently better choices, and in greater transparency.

The responsibility for these choices lies primarily with member governments. That should, however, mean a responsibility shared between executive and legislature, for if members of parliaments take it as part of their duties to monitor and advise on the discharge of their countries' international policies, a part of those duties concerns the quality of the direction of the United Nations system.

Moreover, the United Nations system ultimately belongs to the peoples of the member countries, whom the Charter and all other constitutions pledge to serve. Non-governmental organizations, academic institutions, and individual citizens should also play some part in the process of selecting the leaders of the United Nations and its agencies.

The authors hope that the problems identified in this study, and the recommendations for their remedy, may help all the different partners in the United Nations system to improve its vitality, its performance, and the quality of its service to the international community.

II. RECOMMENDATIONS

▶ Leadership policy for the UN system

Governments should adopt a comprehensive new policy-approach to executive leadership in the United Nations system. The General Assembly should adopt a single comprehensive resolution covering all essential aspects of such a new policy, including term of office, manner of improved selection of the Secretary-General, rules for such appointment, and inviting all other organizations of the system to adopt the same basic policies and procedures including decision to re-phase the timing of appointments of their executive heads to align with that of the Secretary-General in order to facilitate UN-system teamwork.

▶ A UN System Consultative Board

The General Assembly should establish a United Nations System Consultative Board comprising the members of the Bureau of ECOSOC; the Bureaux of the executive governing bodies of the major Specialized Agencies; and one representative of each other Agency. This would provide the essential instrument in which member governments could formulate common policy-approaches on all matters that need the uniform and combined effort of the system.

▶ Terms of office

A standard policy of non-renewable terms of office, and a single seven-year term, should be adopted for all executive-head posts throughout the UN system. If the General Assembly decision is too close to the expiration of a term the incumbent may be invited to accept an appropriate short extension.

▶ Calendar of appointments

The calendar of executive-head appointments should be brought into alignment, so that all heads of the Specialized Agencies would be appointable early in the term of an incoming Secretary-General. By resolution in each governing body the new Secretary-

Brian
Urquhart

Erskine
Childers

A   W O R L D   I N   N E E D
O F   L E A D E R S H I P :
T O M O R R O W ' S   U N I T E D   N A T I O N S
- A   F R E S H   A P P R A I S A L -

General should be consulted on the selection of the next executive head of each Specialized Agency. The timetables of appointments in the system should be re-phased so that they can be made in the second year of the Secretary-General's term.

▶ Search policy

Governments should adopt a common policy that an active search process shall be required for the selection of all executive heads in the UN system, to extend the reservoir of potential candidates beyond those promoting their own nomination, and to ensure that those best qualified are identified.

▶ Proper timetables

For each appointment, dates should be established by which a proper search process shall be launched in a prescribed timetable, which should include a date by which properly constituted nominations must be filed (closing of nominations), and a date by which names of candidates must be circulated.

▶ Vacancy information

Information about each impending vacancy should be circulated through all Member States. Governments should assist the secretariats of the system in making such information available within their countries.

▶ Nominations

Standard rules regarding the filing of nominations should be instituted through the system. These should include the provision by the scheduled date of basic information about a candidate, in a *curriculum vitae* of prescribed maximum length, together with references clearly prescribed.

All nominations to executive-head posts in the system should be forwarded by the Office of the executive President or Prime Minister providing verification of government's endorsement.

▶ Rules of candidature

All candidates and governments should be informed of standard rules. These should include:

- the pledging in advance to any government of any secretariat post, or any other special privilege by a candidate is illegal.
- The pledging *by* any government of additional financial contributions or any other material benefit to the organization if a national is elected is illegal.
- The practice by any member state of any form of economic coercion or suborning to obtain the votes of another member state for any candidate shall result in the election being declared void.
- Campaigning for any executive-head post in the UN system is barred. Staff of an organization should be eligible for consideration but the same prohibition must apply. A staff member who is a candidate and requires from any other staff member any action whatsoever in support, or who uses any other resources of the organization, shall be disqualified.

Governments should adopt provisions for removal from office uniformly throughout the UN system simultaneously with adjusting the term of office.

▶ Search preparation

The senior official responsible for personnel matters in each organization should be specifically charged with assembling and maintaining a well-researched list of outstanding leadership talent for all senior posts up to and including the executive head.

For each vacancy that is filled by an actual election, a special search committee or group should be established by the relevant intergovernmental organ, on a balanced geographical basis. This may itself be intergovernmental, or a special group of eminent persons outside of either government or the UN system. The committee or group should be fully operational, in the case of search for the Secretary-General, not later than the first day of January in the year of appointment, and by an equivalent advance time in the case of other organizations.

The secretariat of the organization concerned should provide a small, high-calibre staff to assist the search committee or group, in strict confidentiality. This staff must be fully assigned and operational not later than the first day of January of the election year or with equivalent time for the work in the case of other organizations. There should be an adequate budget for travel and other communication.

Brian
Urquhart

Erskine
Childers

*A WORLD IN NEED
OF LEADERSHIP:
TOMORROW'S UNITED NATIONS
- A FRESH APPRAISAL -*

▶ *Criteria*

The General Assembly should adopt a statement of the basic qualities to be sought in a Secretary-General. The General Assembly should invite all other governing bodies of the system to follow the example of the World Health Organization in this respect.

The future leaders of the international system should be at the height of their powers and abilities to communicate not least to the young people, in order to shoulder the demanding daily workload and the public responsibilities that a different and highly complex world is going to expect of them.

It would be highly beneficial for the United Nations and for the system as a whole if the next Secretary-General were a woman.

On the eve of the opening of a new appointment process the full-membership deliberative body of each organization of the system should hold a discussion of the kind of leadership that will be needed in the next term of office. Such discussions about the profile of the next leadership period should be conducted in open session and the proceedings should be available to the public. The intergovernmental discussion should be preceded by public hearings.

For the Secretary-Generalship, on 1 January of the appointment year the President of the General Assembly on behalf of the appointive body should issue a public Call for Nominations and Suggestions, stipulating the date by which these should be received, and the method. This should be given widest possible circulation in all Member States.

▶ *Search procedure*

The Search Committee or Group should consult widely throughout the world among governments, parliamentarians, regional groups, former senior national figures and international civil servants, academic institutes and non-governmental organizations. It should examine the qualities, qualifications, personal background and all other pertinent information about all prospective candidates, both those being nominated or informally suggested with valid grounds, and those it may identify. It should have an established progress-reporting timetable.

Fifty per cent of the candidates for executive-head posts finally assembled in each organization's short list should be women.

▶ The Secretary-Generalship

The Search body for the candidate for Secretary-General of the United Nations should, not later than 30 June of the appointment year, provide to the President of the Security Council a short list of not less than 5 and not more than 10 names of highly regarded candidates.

This list should then be circulated publicly, with a further call for comments and further suggestions to be received within 30 days. Member States not members of the Security Council, interested non-governmental bodies, and individuals will thus have a second opportunity to participate in the search process.

At the end of the 30-day period the Search committee or group will resume its work, further investigating already-identified candidates as necessary and any others to whom its attention has been drawn. It will refine its short list by a date stipulated by the Security Council.

Candidates on the refined short list produced by the search process will be further examined by the members of the Security Council. They should be invited to spend some hours discussing their analysis of challenges to be addressed, and their approach to such tasks, and to answer questions. All invited candidates will be offered equal travel and subsistence expenses to enable them to come to UN Headquarters for this purpose.

The Security Council will then proceed to its own deliberations and will submit a recommendation to the General Assembly by an agreed date that will allow sufficient time for the General Assembly to consider the recommendation with due care befitting its appointive responsibility.

The General Assembly may reject a recommendation if the Members judge the candidature inadequate for the tasks of the post, and will then request the Security Council to submit one or more further recommendations until the membership as a whole is satisfied that the General Assembly should proceed to appointment.

In its resolution the General Assembly should invite the Permanent Members of the Security Council to relinquish their vetoes over recommendation for the Secretary-Generalship.

The Security Council should publish a full report of its deliberations and proceedings, including details of all informal and formal votes, so that the process is ultimately placed in the public record. Members of the Search committee or group shall, however, be bound to strict confidentiality.

Brian
Urquhart

Erskine
Childers

A   WORLD   IN   NEED
OF   LEADERSHIP:
TOMORROW'S   UNITED   NATIONS
- A   FRESH   APPRAISAL -

▶ Other organizations

In its establishing resolution on these policies and procedures the General Assembly should invite all other organizations of the system to follow the above approach and search process, including direct examination of short list of candidates, as has been adopted by the World Health Organization.

For executive-head posts in UN funds and programmes the same process should be followed, by a suitable mechanism of the governing body. These proceedings should be accessible to the public either directly or by availability of transcripts.

▶ Organization for effective leadership

The General Assembly should *decide* on the basic organization of the top of the Secretariat, establishing the posts of four Deputy Secretaries-General to head consolidated departments as recommended in this and associated studies.

In the same resolution the General Assembly should further *decide* that all vacancies for senior-echelon posts shall be publicly announced and that all Secretariat positions including all Deputy, USG, ASG and D-2 posts should carry properly prepared and gazetted job descriptions, with the necessary indications to maintain the general geographical and gender balance of the top echelon.

The General Assembly should require that with each announcement of an appointment in the senior echelon the Secretary-General shall describe the appointee's qualifications *in relation to the responsibilities of that specific post.*

The Secretary-General should rapidly achieve a gender balance in the senior echelon, appointment in which is his personal prerogative.

The Secretary-General should implement the General Assembly provision against national monopolies on senior posts, and should be accountable to the General Assembly in this.

The General Assembly should introduce measures to discourage member states from supplementing UN remuneration of its nationals in the Secretariat. It should also seek to remedy the conditions which have motivated this practice in the past.

The equivalent practices should be standard in all other parts of the UN system, in order to bring the system's entire combined senior echelon up to the highest possible levels of quality and appropriateness for its responsibilities. The recommended United Nations System Consultative Board should commission a periodic independent review and evaluation of this echelon, with report to all governing bodies.

▶ **Table 8.** *Past and present executive heads of the UN system*

Organ	Name	Nationality	Term of office	Birth
UN	Trygve Lie	Norway	1946-1953	1896
	Dag Hammarskjöld	Sweden	1953-1961	1905
	U Thant	Burma	1961-1971	1909
	Kurt Waldheim	Austria	1972-1981	1918
	J. Pérez de Cuellar	Peru	1982-1991	1920
	Boutros Boutros-Ghali	Egypt	1992-	1922
UNCHS	A. Ramachandran	India	1978-1994	1923
	Wally S. N'Dow	Gambia	1994-	1943
UNCTAD	Raul Prebisch	Argentina	1965-1969	1901
	Manuel Perez-Guerrero	Venezuela	1969-1974	1911
	Gamani Corea	Sri Lanka	1974-1986	1925
	Kenneth Dadzie	Ghana	1986-1994	1930
	Rubens Ricupero	Brazil	1995-	1937
UNDCP	G. Giacomelli	Italy	1991-	1930
UNDP	Paul Hoffman	USA	1966-1972[1]	1891
	David Owen	UK	1966-1969	1904
	Rudolph Petersen	USA	1972-1976	1904
	Bradford Morse	USA	1976-1986	1921
	W. H. Draper	USA	1986-1993	1928
	James G. Speth	USA	1993-	1942
UNDRO	F. Berkol	Turkey	1972-1982	1917
	M. Essafi	Tunisia	1982-1992	1930
UNEP	Maurice Strong	Canada	1972-1976	1929
	Mustafa Tolba	Egypt	1976-1992	1922
	Elisabeth Dowdeswell	Canada	1992-	1944
UNFPA	Rafael Salas	Philippines	1969-1987	1928
	Nafis Sadik	Pakistan	1987-	1929
UNHCR	G.J. van H. Goedhart	Netherlands	1950-1956	1901
	A.R. Lindt	Switzerland	1956-1960	1905
	F. Schnyder	Switzerland	1960-1965	1910
	Sadruddin Aga Khan	Iran	1965-1977	1933
	P. Hartling	Denmark	1978-1985	1914
	J. Hocke	Switzerland	1985-1989	1938
	T. Stoltenberg	Norway	1990-1992	1931
	Sadako Ogata	Japan	1993-	1927
UNICEF	Maurice Pate	USA	1947-1965	1894
	Henry Labouisse	USA	1965-1979	1904
	James Grant	USA	1980-1995	1922
	Carol Bellamy	USA	1995-	1942

[1] Paul Hoffman was head of the UN Special Fund from 1959 to 1966; David Owen was Chairman of the UN Technical Assistance Board from 1950 to 1966 when these two bodies were merged into the new UNDP; the two men served as co-Administrators of UNDP from 1966 to 1969 when David Owen retired from the UN, and Paul Hoffman continued as sole Administrator until 1972.

Brian
Urquhart

Erskine
Childers

A   W O R L D   I N   N E E D
O F   L E A D E R S H I P :
T O M O R R O W ' S   U N I T E D   N A T I O N S
- A   F R E S H   A P P R A I S A L -

Organ	Name	Nationality	Term of office	Birth
UNITAR	G. d'Arboussier	Senegal	1965-1968	1908
	Simeon Adebo	Nigeria	1968-1972	1913
	Davidson Nicol	Sierra Leone	1972-1982	1924
	M. Doo-Kingue	Cameroon	1982-1992	1934
UNRRA	Herbert Lehman	USA	1943-1946	1878
	Fiorello LaGuardia	USA	Apr.-Dec. 1946	1882
UNRWA	H. Kennedy	Canada	1950-1951	1892
	J. Blanford	USA	1951-1953	1897
	Henry Labouisse	USA	1954-1958	1904
	John H. Davis	USA	1959-1963	1904
	Laurence Michelmore	USA	1964-1971	1909
	Sir John Rennie	UK	1971-1977	1917
	T. McElhiney	USA	1977-1979	1919
	Olof Rydbeck	Sweden	1979-1985	1913
	G. Giacomelli	Italy	1985-1991	1930
	Ilter Turkmen	Turkey	1991-	1927
UNU	J.M. Hester	USA	1975-1980	1924
	Soedjatmoko	Indonesia	1980-1987	1922
	H.G. de Souza	Brazil	1987-	1928
WFC	John Hannah	USA	1975-1978	1902
	Maurice Williams	USA	1978-1986	1920
	G.I. Trant	Canada	1986-	1928
WFP	A.H. Boerma	Netherlands	1962-1967	1912
	F. Aquino	El Salvador	1968-1976	1919
	T.C.M. Robinson	USA	1976-1977	1912
	G.N. Vogel	Canada	1977-1981	1918
	B. de A. Brito Azevedo	Brazil	1981-1982	1935
	J.C. Ingram	Australia	1982-1992	1928
	Catherine A. Bertini	USA	1992-	1950
ILO	E.J. Phelan	Ireland	1941-1948	1888
	David A. Morse	USA	1948-1970	1907
	Wilfred Jenks	UK	1970-1973	1909
	Francis Blanchard	France	1973-1989	1916
	Michel Hansenne	Belgium	1989-	1940
FAO	Sir John Boyd Orr	UK	1945-1948	1880
	Norris E. Dodd	USA	1948-1954	1879
	Philip V. Cardon	USA	1954-1956	1889
	B.R. Sen	India	1956-1967	1898
	A.H. Boerma	Netherlands	1968-1975	1912
	Edouard Saouma	Lebanon	1976-1993	1926
	Jacques Diouf	Senegal	1994-	1926
UNESCO	Julian Huxley	UK	1946-1947	1887
	Jaime T. Bodet	Mexico	1948-1952	1902
	John W. Taylor	USA	1952-1953	1906
	Luther H. Evans	USA	1953-1958	1902
	V. Veronese	Italy	1958-1961	1910
	René Maheu	France	1961-1974	1905
	Amadou M. M'Bow	Senegal	1974-1987	1921
	Federico Mayor	Spain	1987-	1934

Organ	Name	Nationality	Term of office	Birth
ICAO	Albert Roper	France	1946-1951	1891
	E.C.R. Ljungberg	Sweden	1952-1959	1897
	R. McDonnell	Canada	1959-1964	1909
	Bernard T. Twight	Netherlands	1964-1970	1912
	Assad Kotaite	Lebanon	1970-1976	1924
	Yves M. Lambert	France	1976-1988	1936
	S.S. Sidhu	India	1988-1991	1929
	Philippe Rochat	Switzerland	1992-	1942
WHO	Brock Chisholm	Canada	1946-1953	1896
	Marcolino G. Candau	Brazil	1953-1973	1911
	Halfdan T. Mahler	Denmark	1973-1988	1923
	Hiroshi Nakajima	Japan	1988-	1928
UPU	Alois Muri	Switzerland	1945-1949	1879
	Fritz Hess	Switzerland	1950-1960	1895
	Edouard Weber	Switzerland	1961-1966	1901
	Michel Rahi	Egypt	1967-1973	1912
	A.H. Ridge	UK	1973-1974	1913
	M.I. Sobhi	Egypt	1975-1984	1925
	A.C. Botto de Barros	Brazil	1985-1994	1925
	Thomas E. Leavey	USA	1994-	1934
ITU	Franz von Ernst	Switzerland	1947-1950	1879
	Leon Mulatier	France	1950-1953	1887
	M.A. Andrada	Argentina	1954-1958	1904
	Gerald C. Cross	USA	1959-1965	1903
	M.B. Sarwate	India	1965-1967	1910
	Mohamed Mili	Tunisia	1968-1982	1917
	R.E. Butler	Australia	1983-1989	1926
	P.J. Tarjanne	Finland	1989-	1937
WMO	G. Swoboda	Switzerland	1948-1955	1893
	David A. Davies	UK	1955-1980	1913
	A. Wiin-Nielsen	Denmark	1980-1983	1929
	G.O.P. Obasi	Nigeria	1984-	1933
IMO	O.H. Nielsen	Denmark	1959-1961	1893
	J. Roullier	France	1962-1967	1898
	Colin Goad	UK	1968-1973	1914
	C.P. Srivastava	India	1974-1989	1920
	W.A. O'Neil	Canada	1990-	1927
WIPO	Arpad Bogsch	USA	1973-	1919
IFAD	A.M. Al-Sudeary	Saudi Arabia	1980-1984	1936
	Idriss Jazairy	Algeria	1984-1992	1936
	Fawzi H. Al-Sultan	Kuwait	1992-	1944
UNIDO	Domingo Siazon	Philippines	1985-1993	1939
	Mauricio de Maria y Campos	Mexico	1993-	1939
IAEA	Sterling Cole	USA	1957-1961	1904
	Sigvard Eklund	Sweden	1961-1981	1911
	Hans Blix	Sweden	1981-	1928

Brian
Urquhart

Erskine
Childers

*A WORLD IN NEED
OF LEADERSHIP:
TOMORROW'S UNITED NATIONS
- A FRESH APPRAISAL -*

Organ	Name	Nationality	Term of office	Birth
GATT	Eric W. White	UK	1948-1968	1913
	Olivier Long	Switzerland	1968-1980	1915
	Arthur Dunkel	Switzerland	1980-1993	1932
	Peter Sutherland	Ireland	1993-1994	1946
WTO	Renato Ruggiero	Italy	1995-	1930
IBRD	Eugene Mayer	USA	June-Dec. 1946	1876
	John McCloy	USA	1947-1949	1895
	Eugene R. Black	USA	1949-1962	1898
	George D. Woods	USA	1963-1968	1901
	Robert McNamara	USA	1968-1981	1916
	A.W. Clausen	USA	1981-1986	1923
	Barber B. Conable	USA	1986-1991	1922
	Lewis T. Preston	USA	1991-1995	1926
	James D. Wolfensohn	USA	1995-	1933
IMF	Camille Gutt	Belgium	1946-1951	1884
	Ivar Rooth	Sweden	1951-1956	1888
	Per Jacobsson	Sweden	1956-1963	1894
	Pierre-Paul Schweitzer	France	1963-1973	1912
	H. J. Witteveen	Netherlands	1973-1978	1921
	J. deLarosière	France	1978-1986	1929
	Jean-Michel Camdessus	France	1987-	1933

▶ Glossary of Abbreviations *

UN	United Nations: the central organization
UN S-G	Secretary-General of the United Nations
UNCHS	United Nations Centre for Human Settlements
UNCTAD	United Nations Conference on Trade and Development
UNDCP	United Nations Drug Control Programme
UNDP	United Nations Development Programme
UNDRO	United Nations Disaster Relief Office
UNEP	United Nations Environment Programme
UNFPA	United Nations Population Fund
UNHCR	United Nations Office of High Commissioner for Refugees
UNICEF	United Nations Children's Fund
UNITAR	United Nations Institute for Training and Research
UNRRA **	United Nations Relief and Rehabilitation Administration
UNRWA	United Nations Relief and Works Agency for Palestine Refugees
UNU	United Nations University
WFC	World Food Council
WFP	World Food Programme
IAEA	International Atomic Energy Agency
ILO	International Labour Organization
FAO	Food and Agriculture Organization of the United Nations
UNESCO	United Nations Educational, Scientific and Cultural Organization
WHO	World Health Organization
IBRD	International Bank for Reconstruction and Development (World Bank)
IMF	International Monetary Fund
ICAO	International Civil Aviation Organization
UPU	Universal Postal Union
ITU	International Telecommunications Union
WMO	World Meteorological Organization
IMO	International Maritime Organization
WIPO	World Intellectual Property Organization
IFAD	International Fund for Agricultural Development
UNIDO	United Nations Industrial Development Organization
GATT***	General Agreement on Tariffs and Trade
WTO ***	World Trade Organization

*   Organizations referred to in text or tables
**   No longer in existence but part of leadership history
*** The GATT had cooperation with the United Nations but was not a Specialized Agency. It has been replaced by the WTO, which has not to date been brought into relationship with the UN as a Specialized Agency.

INDEX

Legend: S-G = Secretary-General; D-G = Director-General of a Specialized Agency;
GA = General Assembly; SC = Security Council

Brian
Urquhart

Erskine
Childers

A   WORLD   IN   NEED
OF   LEADERSHIP:
TOMORROW'S   UNITED   NATIONS
- A   FRESH   APPRAISAL -

101

Authors and Sponsors

Brian Urquhart,
formerly Scholar-in-Residence in the International Affairs Program at the Ford Foundation, was one of the first United Nations civil servants, and served in the United Nations Secretariat from 1945 until his retirement in 1986. He worked closely with the first five Secretaries-General on peace and security matters, especially peace-keeping, and was Under Secretary-General for Special Political Affairs from 1974 to 1986. He is the author of *Hammarskjold*, a biography of the second Secretary-General, *A Life in Peace and War, Decolonization and World Peace*, and most recently, *Ralph Bunche: An American Life*.

Erskine Childers
(Ireland) currently Secretary–General of the World Federation of United Nations Associations (WFUNA), retired in 1989 as Senior Adviser to the UN Director–General for Development and International Economic Co–operation after 22 years as a UN civil servant. Before 1967 he was a writer, lecturer and broadcaster on international political and development affairs, specializing in UN issues and serving as a periodic consultant including a special mission in the Congo for Secretary–General U Thant. He has worked with most of the organizations of the system at all levels and in all regions. His books include *The Road to Suez: A Study in Western–Arab Relations* and most recently he was Academic Editor of *Challenges to the United Nations*.

The Dag Hammarskjöld Foundation was established in 1962 in memory of the late Secretary-General of the United Nations. It is an operating, not a grant-making foundation, and its main purpose is to organize seminars and conferences on the social, economic, legal and cultural issues facing the Third World and to publish the materials arising from these activities.

The Ford Foundation is a private philanthropic institution dedicated to international peace and to advancing the well-being of people throughout the world. Under the policy guidance of a Board of Trustees the Foundation grants and lends funds for educational, developmental, research, and experimental efforts designed to produce significant advances on problems of world-wide importance.